DENNIS
100 YEARS OF INNOVATION
Stewart J. Brown

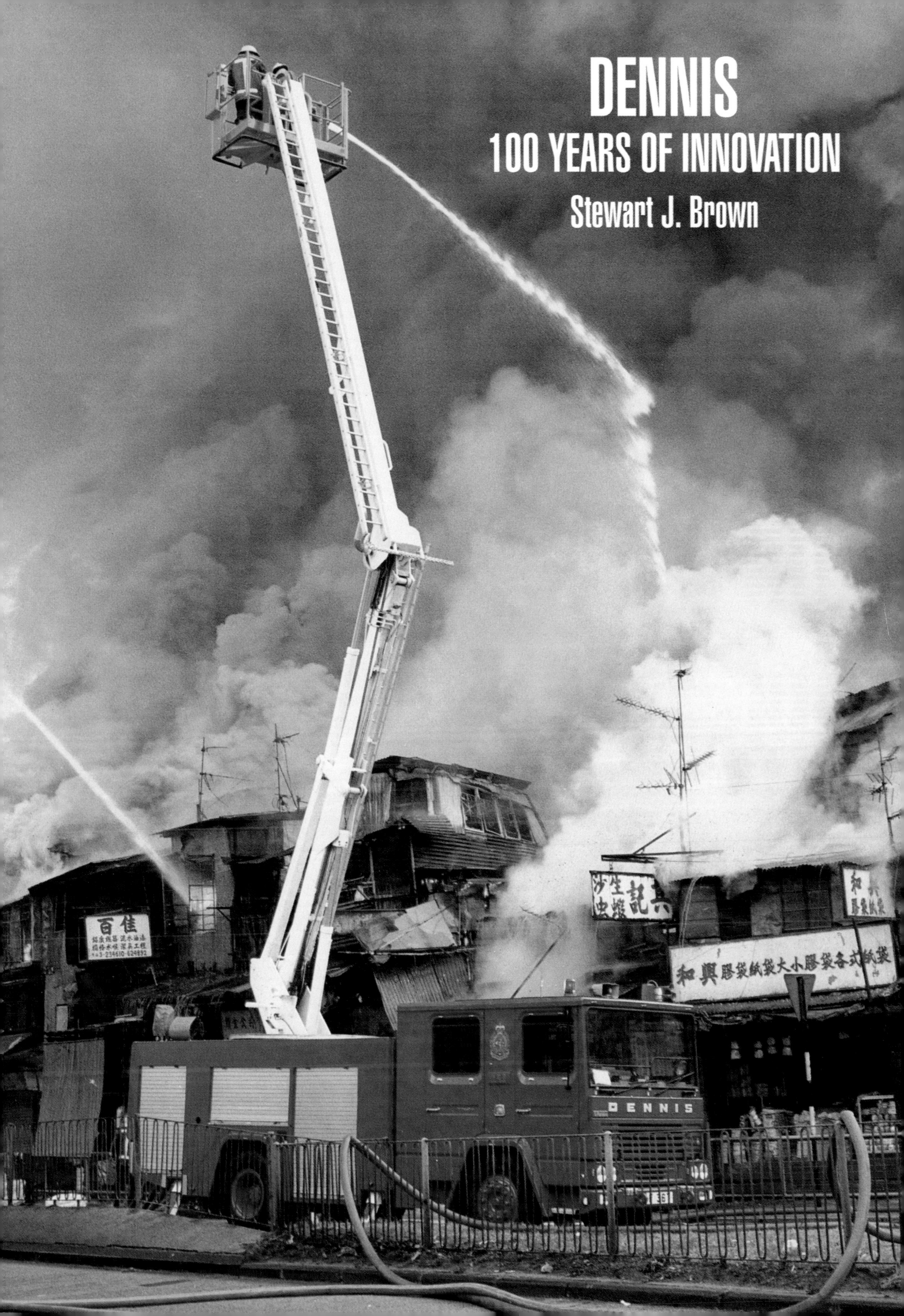

INVICTA
INVICTA
INVICTA
INVICTA
DENNIS
DENNIS
RBT·206
RBT·200
RBT·204
VOLGREN

IAN ALLAN Publishing

DENNIS

100 YEARS OF INNOVATION

Stewart J. Brown

DENNIS

100 YEARS OF INNOVATION

Stewart J. Brown

First published 1995

ISBN 0 7110 2322 0

Published by Ian Allan Publishing

an imprint of Ian Allan Ltd, Terminal House, Station Approach, Shepperton, Surrey TW17 8AS.

Printed by Ian Allan Printing Ltd, Coombelands House, Coombelands Lane, Addlestone, Weybridge, Surrey KT15 1HY.

Acknowledgements

A number of people have to be thanked in helping with the production of this book. Dennis directors John Smith, Roger Heard and Vernon Edwards all made their time and knowledge available. Also at Dennis, Bob Loveland provided invaluable information and has over the years played a key part in ensuring the preservation of a healthy Dennis archive.

The archive material is kept by Surrey County Council's record office and thanks have to be made to Maggie Vaughan-Lewis and her team at the Guildford Muniment Room and in particular Lawrence Spring who has documented the Dennis material.

Unless otherwise credited all photographs come from either the Dennis archive or the author's collection. Individual photographers who have helped out with photographs are: Gavin Booth, Peter Davies, Peter Durham, Michael Fowler, Michael Grieves, Charles F. Klapper and Roger Pennington.

Stewart J. Brown
Framilode
1995

Contents

Introduction

The occasion of our centenary has caused many of the present team at Dennis to look at the history of the business, and to ask themselves why Dennis should not only have survived from those early days but be prospering to the degree that it is. In our centenary year we are the market leaders in all our chosen fields of vehicle manufacture: Public Service, Municipal and Emergency vehicles. How has this wholly British company survived when so many of our competitors have either been swallowed up by foreign competitors or ceased to exist altogether?

The answer, I believe, is threefold. Firstly Dennis' products have been highly innovative from the very beginning, as the reader will discover upon examining the contents of this book.

As the company's fortunes ebbed and flowed over the years, just when all seemed lost a new product emerged to restart the momentum of the business. This happened after World War 1, and again in recent times with the Phoenix refuse collection vehicle, the RS and SS fire engine range, the Javelin coach chassis and latterly the Dart midibus chassis, which have all combined to propel the company to its present dominance.

Secondly Dennis has always remained very close to its customers; almost always selling products directly to the end user, thereby knowing his or her needs and aspirations at first hand. I would like to take this opportunity of thanking all our customers who have supported us throughout the years of our existence. Many of our earliest customers, particularly in the Fire and Municipal field, are with us to this day, and it was they, together with our Bus customers, who saw the company through its lean years.

Finally, and most importantly, the success of the business has been achieved through the contribution made by its employees. As today's Managing Director I am merely the custodian of a long tradition; and I would like to pay tribute and thanks to the energy and dedication of those who work for the company. This transmits itself into an extraordinary loyalty and enthusiasm for the marque, Dennis, whether by employee, customer or supplier.

With exciting new products in the pipeline, and plans for further overseas development I feel Dennis can look forward with confidence to the future both in Britain and abroad, and to a successful second century.

John I. Smith
Managing Director

Picture: **Roger Pennington**

In the Beginning

Enthusiastic vehicle engineers

n 1895 Queen Victoria ruled over an Empire on which the sun never set. She had reigned since 1837, and was to do so until her death in 1901 at the age of 81. During her reign Britain had changed rapidly, from an agricultural land to the workshop of the world.

The industrial revolution had gathered pace in the second half of the 19th century and with it had come significant advances in transport. For long-distance transport - which effectively meant anything more than about 25 miles - an intensive railway network moved both goods and people.

But that was about to change. Rail transport's supremacy was about to be successfully challenged by a new form of road transport - cars, lorries and buses powered by the new-fangled internal combustion engine.

Far-sighted as John Dennis might have

In presenting this Catalogue of our Motor Cars to the public, we wish to thank our many clients for the support they have favoured us with in the past.

As the oldest manufacturer of Motor Vehicles in this country, we have the advantage of past experience in Motor Construction, and through persistent and careful attention to every detail we have been able to keep the lead.

In placing before you our 1906 Models, we have combined experience with the highest possible skilled labour, supported by probably the largest and best equipped factory engaged entirely in Motor Car Construction today.
— *introduction to 1906 brochure*

Left: **Cover of 1912 brochure. At this time Dennis production was concentrated on cars.**

Above: **The men behind the name: Raymond *(top)* and John Dennis *(above).***

been, the idea of vehicle production was most certainly not in his mind when in 1894 he left his native Devon to join a firm of ironmongers in Guildford. John had been brought up in rural Huntsham, a few miles from Tiverton, but his real interest was more in farm machinery than in farming.

He was 23 when he arrived in Guildford, and in his spare time built a bicycle which he sold at a profit. More followed, and at the start of 1895 he gave up his job with the ironmonger and set up his own business. This was The Universal Athletic Stores in Guildford's High Street, and from it he sold his Speed Queen and Speed King bicycles for ladies and gentlemen. It was clear to John from his success as a part-time cycle-maker that this new venture was bound to succeed - and his younger brother, Raymond, then aged 17, moved up from Devon to join him in this expanding enterprise.

The new business did succeed, to the extent that a proper workshop was built behind the shop to manufacture bicycles and tricycles.

In 1898 the brothers, already sensing the way things would go, produced their first motorised vehicle, a tricycle fitted with a single-cylinder French-built De Dion engine. The frame had to be strengthened to carry the extra weight, but this primitive machine worked reasonably well - and caused John Dennis to fall foul of the law.

There was little point in having a powered tricycle if you weren't going to use it, and John was apprehended while putting it through its paces. He was prosecuted for "driving furiously up Guildford High Street at 16mph". If his rudimentary tricycle really was doing 16mph up Guildford High Street - which is fairly steep - it was quite an achievement. This escapade brought a fine of 20 shillings but was quickly turned to Dennis's advantage when advertisments for the new Dennis motor tricycle quoted the incident as proof of the machine's rapidity. Then as now, speed was a selling point for many motorists.

By the end of the century Dennis was building motorised quadricycles as well as tricycles. The quadricycle used bicycle-type framing which was light and offered minimal comfort, rather than the more solid engineering associated with purpose-designed motor cars. The 3½hp engine was mounted at the rear, steering was by a tiller, rather than a wheel. A one- or two-seat trailer was available as an option.

But the motor car wasn't far off. In 1900 the company moved to bigger premises in Guildford's North Street - an old army barracks - and in 1901 produced its first car. Like the tricycles and quadricycles, power was provided by a tried and tested De Dion single-cylinder

> Whatever the opinion of Motor Constructors may be, we may assert here at once that the Worm Drive Dennis Motor Omnibus is quite the quietest and sweetest drive of its kind we have yet encountered, and as the interior of a half-loaded Motor'Bus is the place to experience the characteristics of such a drive, we do not speak without our book. Sweetness and quietude are the special features of the Worm Drive Dennis Vehicles.
> — *from a report in* Motor Traction, *1905*

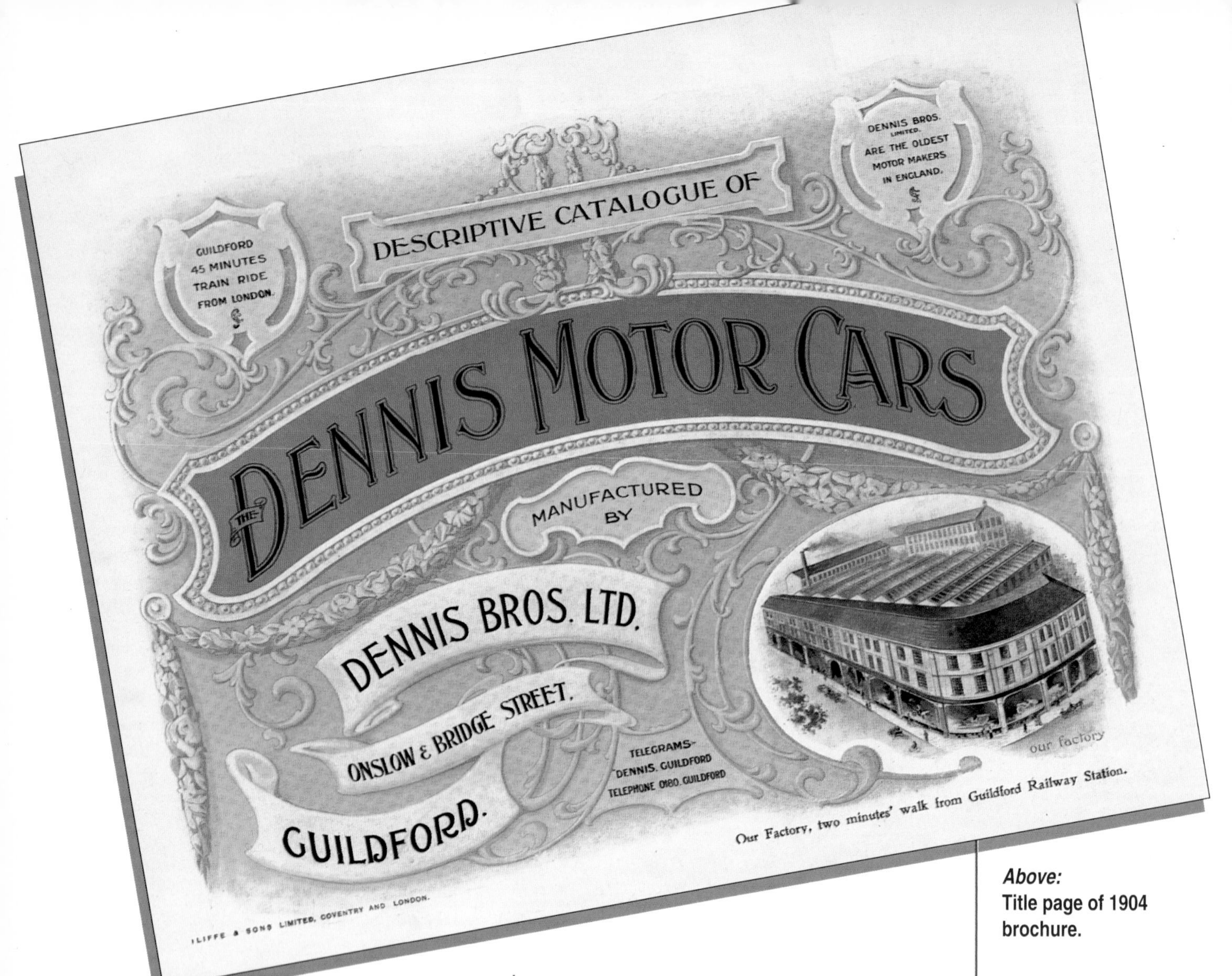

Above:
Title page of 1904 brochure.

engine mounted at the front, and of 8hp output rather than the 3½hp of the lighter vehicles. A three-speed gearbox was fitted. A 10hp two-cylinder model was soon added to the range.

Prices in 1902 were:

8hp car	280 guineas
10hp car	320 guineas
3hp quadricycle	115 guineas
3hp tricycle	82 guineas
Dennis trailer	£20

Motor cars were still quite a novelty in 1901, with probably fewer than 500 on Britain's roads. Most road traffic was horse drawn. There was a growing number of manufacturers in Britain, most of them very small, and each looking for the best ways of extolling the advantages of their products over those of their rivals.

One of the accepted ways of doing this was to take part in reliability trials, and this was an opportunity which the Dennis brothers were quick to seize. In 1901 a Dennis won first prize in the Tilburstow Hill Climb, and this was followed by success for two cars in a non-stop run from London to Oxford. The distance of 60 miles may not sound like much of a challenge the best part of a century later, but it was a significant achievement. In the Automobile Club's 1,000-mile trial in 1903 a Dennis car completed the course with flying colours. Out of 65 starters, only 23 made it

> The Cannes season is beginning in earnest. The Grand Duke Michael of Russia and Countess Torby, who are hospitably entertaining, as usual, at the Villa Kasbeck, often drive down to the golf links in their new Dennis Motor Car, which has just arrived from England, and is an excellent example of British workmanship.
> — *from a report in the* Daily Mail, *1904*

Above:
In 1901 the company moved to a new factory and showroom in North Street. The building still stands.

back to London's Marble Arch.

These were exciting times. Motoring was growing in popularity, but it was an expensive pastime and there was no guarantee that it would really catch on. There were very real concerns about dangers to pedestrians and animals, and many early machines were highly unreliable. Roads were generally poorly surfaced, and quite inadequate for the new generation of relatively high-speed vehicles, which could legally travel at 20mph from 1903.

> All orders are executed strictly in rotation as received; we cannot under any consideration deviate from this rule. Prospective buyers are cordially invited to satisfy themselves thoroughly by making a practical road trial of our cars before placing their orders.
>
> An instructor is sent free of charge for one week with each retail customer, provided his board and lodgings are paid for. We send, to the best of our knowledge, reliable drivers, but customers must accept them without holding us in any way liable for their inefficiency.
>
> — *from 1906 terms of business*

But the Dennis brothers had faith. A private limited company - Dennis Brothers Ltd - was set up with £30,000 share capital in 1901, and such was the interest in the company's products that further expansion quickly followed with a new office and factory in Onslow Street. This was described in a 1902 issue of *The Gentleman's Journal* as 'one of the handsomest buildings in Surrey'.

Vehicles were developing quickly, too. In 1903 Dennis introduced its worm-drive rear axle, arguably the first British motor manufacturer to do so. This was quieter, more efficient and more reliable than the chain drive commonly in use at the beginning of the century. As vehicles became more robust, Dennis looked at ways of increasing sales. There was, after all, only a limited number of landed gentry with the time and the money to play with motorised transport.

The question in the minds of Dennis and a number of other early manufacturers looking to expand sales was a simple one: could the motor car be adapted to bring benefits to businesses which were reliant on horse-drawn transport? The answer was yes, and in 1904 Dennis built its first commercial vehicle, a 15cwt van for London's most famous department store - Harrods. This had a two-cylinder 12hp De Dion engine and was exhibited at the Crystal Palace Motor Show. The engine was mounted in a separate sub-frame, designed to reduce the stress on the chassis.

In the same year the first Dennis bus took to the streets. This had a longer wheelbase and a 28hp Aster engine. It was supplied to one Benjamin Richardson for operation between Kingston-on-Thames and Richmond. Further bus orders soon followed from the Mid-Sussex Motor Syndicate and from Thomas Tilling.

With a broader range of products - cars, light commercial vehicles and buses - Dennis Brothers needed still more space. A new 10 acre site was purchased at Woodbridge Hill on the edge of Guildford, a site which was to be the company's home for the best part of 90 years. One of the first buildings on the new site was the former Torrey Alexander Mission Hall from Brixton, south London. This was dismantled, transported the 30 or so miles to Guildford, and re-erected at Woodbridge where it later became known as No1 shop. It provided some 25,000 sq ft of working space.

Publicity was still being won by performances in events of various sorts. In 1905 John Dennis and Reginald Downing drove two 14hp Dennis cars in the Tourist Trophy, coming 16th and 18th out of 42 starters. Downing had joined the company in 1902, and was to become a director in 1913 and to remain on the board until 1955. In 1906 a 20hp model completed 4,007 miles in an Automobile Club trial, which won the company the first-ever Dewar Trophy. "The entire absence of wear astounded the judges," said Dennis. In the following year a 2-ton van won a silver medal in trials organised by the Royal Automobile Club, as it was now known.

The 20hp, and the broadly similar 24hp, were offered with a choice of bodies - Phaeton, Brougham, Landaulette and Waggonette at prices in the £700 to £800 bracket. The lighter 14hp sold for between £400 and £575.

The balance of production was changing slowly, with fewer cars but more commercial vehicles being built. Most of these were trucks and vans - all straightforward four-wheelers - along with a few buses. The new Woodbridge factory concentrated on bigger models, production of which was increasing rapidly,

Below:
The oldest surviving Dennis car — a 1902 model. *Roger Pennington*

Above:
The Dennis Hansom which sold for 500 guineas in 1904. It was powered by a two-cylinder engine.

Right:
The Dennis Taxi Cab in 1912; it had a cone clutch, an 18hp four-cylinder engine and the company's patented worm-drive axle.

while cars and light commercials were built in Onslow Street. There were two main car models, a 20hp which sold for £600, and a 30-35hp for £700.

The comprehensive tool kit which came with a 45hp model added to the range in 1907 gives an indication of the resourcefulness expected of the Edwardian motorist, or from his or her man. Supplied in a roll-up leather case it comprised:

2 box spanners
2 screwdrivers
2 pliers
1 hammer
2 engine spanners
1 spark plug spanner
1 carburettor key
1 each small and large adjustable spanners
1 file
1 oilcan
1 petrol funnel
2 spark plugs
1 repairing outfit with
2 tyre levers
2 tube spanners
1 grip wrench
1 hand vice
1 punch
spare bolts and nuts
split pins
taper pins
insulation tape
copper and asbestos washers
asbestos string
1ft steam hose pipe
4 sparking plug washers
2 hose pipe clips
1 pump
1 brass or nickel plated horn.

At the 1907 Olympia show Dennis had on display a new 40hp bus chassis, a complete 35hp 34-seat bus, a 40hp 4-ton brewer's lorry, a 20hp 2-ton lorry and a 20hp 2-ton van. New was an express van which could carry 30cwt at 18mph. Dennis described its products in an advert for the show as 'All a marvel of Engineering Skill'. Which, no doubt, they were.

The company was anxious to prove that its products were economical, and published figures showing the costs involved in running a 2½-ton Dennis van for 60 miles a day for five days plus 30 miles on Saturdays - a total of 330 miles a week which was quite a respectable figure for an early delivery van. The figures were:

"Dennis" Patent Rear Axle with Worm Gear

(PATENT No. 3224)

GEARING GUARANTEED FOR TWO YEARS

We are the pioneers of worm gear with horizontal drive from the gear box, and at the time of our adopting this principle the system was denounced on all sides, both by engineers and by rival firms. That we were right is proved by the great efficiency the worm gear provides to-day, and we are further supported by the fact that all the best firms in repute are adopting it. A car to-day is out of date which has not got worm gear fitted.

To make a worm gear axle requires both experience and great accuracy. It is possible, as we have proved, to make a worm pinion and wheel of such material, cut them at such an angle and pitch that, when mounted on bearings above suspicion, the friction between the two surfaces is even less than spur gear and considerably less than chain or bevel gear, with the additional advantage of being absolutely silent in action.

The efficiency of the worm gear is equally displayed, whether the worm pinion is driving the worm wheel or the worm wheel is driving the pinion; there is not the slightest tendency towards irreversibility.

The worm gear is contained in a specially constructed differential gear box, and runs at each end on most efficient large ball journal and thrust bearings. The worm wheel encircles the differential gear, which is of the parallel pinion type, with six pinions and two star pinions.

The rear axle casing is a malleable casting with strengthened flanges into which are screwed and locked the live axle casings. These casings extend and take up the bearing of the road wheels, which in turn take up the drive through driving stars, engaging with the square end of the live axles and fitting into recesses on the rear hubs.

It will be observed that the wheels have an independent ball bearing with which to support the weight of the car with its passengers, and the live axle has to transmit the drive only.

The lubrication is perfect, because the worm wheel is naturally formed to pick up the clean oil, and consequently lubricate the worm pinion. If there is any dirt in the oil, it naturally falls to the bottom of the case, and is not circulated by the worm wheel, which only dips the clean oil on the surface.

There is a further great advantage by using a horizontal drive, and that is the greater efficiency through relieving the universal joints of any strain.

Observe the Driving Axle and Worm Pinion supported on large diameter Compound Ball Journal and Thrust Bearings.

26

Above:
Thomas Tilling was an early Dennis customer. This double-deck bus for operation in London is seen at the 1911 Olympia show.

Left:
Dennis was a pioneer in the use of a worm-drive rear axle and it came with a two-year guarantee. 'A car today is out of date which has not got worm gear fitted,' said a contemporary Dennis brochure.

Petrol, 8mpg at 1s 2d	£2 6s 5½d
Cylinder oil, 80mpg at 1s 4d	5s 4d
Depreciation,	
15 per cent per annum	£1 16s 4d
Repairs, average	15s 0d
Tyres,	
10,000 miles, £40 per set	£1 6s 8d
Interest on outlay at	
5 per cent per annum	12s 1d
Insurance,	
£15 per annum	5s 9d
Driver's wages	£1 10s 0d
Total	£8 17s 7½d

This equalled 2½d per ton mile.

The tyres, incidentally, solids at this time, carried a 10,000 mile guarantee.

A model which was to significantly alter the company's future direction was built in 1908. It was a fire engine for the City of Bradford Fire Brigade. At this time most fire engines were horse drawn and had steam-powered pumps, a combination which was far from efficient for an emergency service. However it was all that was available.

The Bradford fire engine, a 45hp model costing £900, used a four-cylinder White and Poppe engine to give more power than was available from the Aster engines being used in the rest of the Dennis range. This not only drove the fire engine (by way of a worm drive axle of course) but, through a power take off, drove the Gwynne-Sargeant turbine pump. Or, in the words of the *Colliery Guardian*, the engine was 'not only for purposes of locomotion, but also for pumping'.

The Bradford appliance attracted a lot of attention, and added fuel to the debate about the best ways of getting to fires quickly - horse or motor vehicle. The argument was short-lived. The days of the horse-drawn fire appliance were numbered and brigades throughout Britain bought Dennis fire appliances in quite considerable numbers.

Above:
Another bus customer in the early days was Aldershot & District. Dennis chassis played a major part in the A&D fleet for over 50 years.

White and Poppe, based in Coventry, soon became the main supplier of engines across all Dennis models, cars included.

Not all innovation was as successful as the fire engine. A spin-off from the fire-engine development - insofar as it used a power take off to drive a pump - was the Dennis agricultural and irrigation machine. It was perhaps surprising, in view of the Dennis brothers' background in rural Devon, that they had not thought earlier about applying some of their expertise to farm equipment. The new machine, announced in the summer of 1909, could plough two furrows, drive a 4ft 6in threshing machine and deliver 250 gallons per minute to a height of 20ft. It was perhaps too versatile for its own good, in an area of business activity which had long been conservative. Few, if any, were built after the prototype, which was sold to a sugar plantation in Natal.

But the company's mainstream activities

Enquiries about the firm whose car you buy

This precaution is very necessary in the present position of the Motor Industry, now that the supply is as great as the demand. There are a large number of mushroom firms, with no backbone whatsoever, and who have been trading upon the deposits received from their clients; such firms cannot last, and if you find yourself the possessor of a Car made by such a firm, or the possessor of a Car imported by the so-called Sole Concessionaire who has had to suspend business, then you have made a very inadvisable purchase, both because of the difficulty to obtain spare parts, and, the name not being kept constantly before the public, any reputation the car may have soon goes and with it your chance of re-sale except at a considerable sacrifice.

Nothing speaks so highly of the business ability of a Company, or the goods they manufacture, as consistent and steady advancement, and, without exception, our progress has been unparalleled in the history of the Motor Trade. We commenced manufacturing before the passing of the Light Locomotive Act, which gives us the position of the oldest Makers in England, and we have battled with every stage of the Industry.

— *introduction to 1908 brochure*

Above:
Car production was given up in favour of trucks and one of the most successful was the subvention model. This impressive specimen was for a bakery in Essex.

continued to thrive. Orders for buses and charabancs were coming in from around the country, and there was export business too, with buses going to Russia and New Zealand. Indeed with continuing high interest in the company's heavier vehicles it felt obliged to issue a statement in 1909 to confirm that it was still building 'pleasure cars'. Customers for these included a Brazilian Viscount and Grand Duke Michael of Russia. The company also sold second-hand Dennis cars for a short time.

A spin-off from the car business was a taxi-cab, and Dennis supplied cabs to Portugal and Australia. Nearer home they were also running in Cardiff, Dundee and Oxford.

The motorised fire engine was winning new business too. One was delivered to Glasgow in 1909 (being transported by sea) and was the city's first motorised fire appliance. The first of a long line of Dennises for the London Fire Brigade took to the capital's streets in 1910. When Lanarkshire County Council inaugurated its fire brigade in 1911, three Dennises were used. Lanarkshire claimed: 'It is calculated that all important populous places can be reached by the motor engines within 15 minutes of the receipt of the call; also, in the case of large country houses and mansions, provided a telephone connection exists, these should be reached in well under the half hour'. Fire engines, too, were being exported, with a veritable A to Z of customers quickly building

> The Crystal Palace Exhibition of motor cars has been very successful, one firm, Messrs. Dennis Bros., Ltd., of Guildford, having taken orders for over £30,000 worth.
> — Daily Express *report, 1903*

up, from Auckland to Zanzibar.

Although the horseless fire brigade was coming, things didn't always go smoothly as brigades adapted to the new techniques involved in running motor vehicles. In 1911 the Kings Heath Fire Brigade, near Birmingham, was involved in a fatal accident when it was testing its new 40hp Dennis, which skidded on a wet road, throwing off a crew member who was killed. The driver was quoted in the *Birmingham Evening Dispatch* as saying: 'The engine suddenly gave a great swerve, almost turning round, and dashed straight into the fence, which is of very stout construction.'

Dennis lorries were also making their mark abroad, and early export markets included Egypt and Cyprus. At home the company claimed in 1910 that there were 200 firms running over 1,000 Dennis lorries and vans - adding as a comment on the designs which had achieved such success 'the chief desideratum is simplicity'.

The flexibility to produce specialised vehicles, a hallmark of Dennis for most of its existence, was evident before World War I. Although it had a standard range of chassis, it could still produce vehicles designed for specific uses. An early example was a 5-ton 35hp pantechnicon chassis on which the frame was widened behind the rear axle to help loading by furniture removal companies.

And, demonstrating that there's nothing new under the sun, the prototype pantechnicon was fitted with a Jurus recorder which showed speeds and times on a continuous strip of specially-prepared paper in a sealed box. The Jurus, a primitive tachograph, was driven from the front wheels and had an eight-day clock.

Dennis offered a wide range of bodywork on its commercial vehicle chassis, all produced in its own bodyshops. On the 35hp model a 34-seat double-deck bus body cost £150. On the 28hp model a 16-seat single-decker was £120, while a 20-seat charabanc was £100. The 35hp chassis cost £650 - so a complete

Above:
Motorised transport could still draw crowds in the days before World War 1, as these two buses outside London's Fenchurch Street station while on delivery to the Southend on Sea & District Motor Omnibus Co show.

Drivers are warned to examine their brakes each morning before starting and find out whether they are holding sufficiently or require adjustment, as it is courting disaster to drive a car with defective brake power. Our pattern brakes are of large diameter and require little adjustment, which can easily be effected in two minutes.
— *from* Hints to Drivers, *in brochure c1904*

Above:
An early fire engine and its crew posed outside the fire station — or engine house as it was then known — at Guildford. Machines such as this established Dennis's reputation as a supplier of safe and reliable fire appliances.

double-decker was £800 - while the 28hp chassis was £585. Both were also offered with lorry bodies. The 18hp motor van chassis (£435) could be supplied with a van body (£50), as a Traveller's Brougham (£90), with a tower wagon body (£65) or with an ambulance body 'painted and finished in first-rate style' at an expensive-sounding £100.

For the tough conditions found in export markets, an 18hp Colonial car was developed. Compared with the standard model it had a stronger frame, longer springs, bigger wheels made of steel instead of wood, a larger radiator, and the carburettor located on top of the engine to minimise the risk of the engine cutting out when driving through deep water. This inventiveness was rewarded with an immediate order for 25 from South Africa.

Special bodies on standard chassis included a hearse on a 5cwt goods model, and a Black Maria for operation in Salford, built on a 35hp chassis.

As the popularity of motor vehicles increased, so Dennis expanded to cope with growing demand for its products, which were highly regarded. Indeed in 1909 *The Autocar* was moved to say: 'Private cars or commercial vehicles, motor fire engines or motor ploughs, when found bearing the name plate of Messrs Dennis Bros of Guildford, are now recognised as among the best automobile engineering outputs in this country... Their pleasure cars and utilitarian motor vehicles stand second to none.'

The Woodbridge site was growing, with No2 shop in 1910, No3 in 1911 and No4 in 1912, by which time the company was claiming an annual output of 1,000 vehicles from its 'large fleet of workmen'. No2 had to be extended in 1914 by which time the four shops offered some 137,000sq ft of production space. This was almost doubled in 1916 when shops 5, 6 and 7 were erected with a further 124,000 sq ft of space. The workforce doubled

Dennis

P·8A1
Dennis

Left:
An Edwardian touring car from the Dennis range.

Below Left:
A 35hp chassis which was tested at Brooklands and covered 5.25 miles in four minutes and 30sec — which works out at 70mph.

from just over 400 in 1909 to over 800 during World War I. The Onslow Street site was retained as a repair shop.

Around this time the company built its own power house with four massive low-revving Sulzer diesel engines. These had flywheels 10ft in diameter and weighing 10 tons and the engines turned over at a remarkable 120rpm. These engines were to be long-lived, and 60 years later were still earning their keep.

To fund all this growth a new public company with £300,000 of capital was formed - Dennis Brothers (1913) Ltd. John and Raymond Dennis were directors, along with Reg Downing, George Suter and Herbert Dawes. The first chairman was George Clare, who was succeeded in 1914 by Nicholas Andrew.

The new company re-appraised its goals. War was in the air. Demand for commercial vehicles was growing steadily, and it was a market in which Dennis was making its mark. It was also a market where there were a comparatively small number of strong players - in marked contrast to the car business which was much more competitive. Dennis decided to develop a new strategy, which would see it concentrating on lorries, fire engines and buses. Car production ceased in 1913; the final models were four-cylinder 15.9hp and 24hp types.

World War 1
Excellence through innovation

Left:
Typical of the fire engines being built when the company decided to concentrate on heavy vehicle production is this appliance delivered to Coventry Fire Brigade in 1914. When new it had solid tyres.

he winding up of car production left Dennis free to concentrate on lorries, buses and fire engines. As war approached, lorries assumed growing importance.

The British government had recognised a few years before war broke out that there was a strong chance that it would. It also recognised that in the event of war, motorised transport could play a significant part in deciding victory. What it didn't want when war came was to find itself commandeering from civilian users a rag-bag selection of lorries of widely differing designs and reliability standards. So it devised a plan to encourage the use of certain makers' products where these were of proven reliability and durability.

Under the subvention or subsidy scheme, the owner of an appropriate lorry which was properly maintained and would be available for requisition in the event of war received a payment of £110, paid in three annual instalments. The advantage to the vehicle owner was that not only did he receive a cash payment, but he had the security of knowing that the lorry he was buying had passed the War Department's rigorous tests. Which was quite a valuable endorsement for any product.

A Dennis brochure on the subject advised: 'The only inconvenience entailed is the necessity for allowing the vehicle to be inspected once every six months by an expert representing the War Department. This inspection is carried out with a minimum of inconvenience to the owner, and serves to assure you that your lorry is being skilfully driven and properly maintained by your employees.'

Dennis submitted 3-ton lorries for approval, which they got without too much trouble. The War Department required that the lorries be able to work for long periods without overheating, which required changes to the radiator and saw Dennis finally abandon Aster engines and standardise on White and Poppe units. Dennis was one of a number of manufacturers to submit lorries for approval under the subvention scheme. Others who did, and were accepted, included AEC, Leyland, Maudslay, Thornycroft and Commercial Cars. Dennis built over 7,000 of its subvention model between 1914 and 1918. Production was running at over 20 a week, and peaked at over 30. They proved reliable in the tough conditions they had to face — the first major war in which motor vehicles played a significant part.

It was a tough test and showed just how much designs had advanced in a decade. One Private Gordon, of No1 Ammunition Park, Army Service Corps, who it would seem couldn't have had much else on his mind at the start of 1915, had this to say of them in a letter: 'Well, to let you know how the Dennises are running. To speak the truth, I cannot say anything bad about them. Troubles are very few and back axles are excellent: I have not heard of one going yet. We get fairly big loads and very bad roads to travel on. For miles we get cobbles, and I must say the Dennis is one of the best we have out here.'

Above:
Charabancs such as this, delivered to a Carlisle operator, Percivals, opened up the countryside. It is built on a 3-ton chassis.
Robert Grieves Collection.

Dennis made other contributions to the war effort. It supplied a pumping set to deliver drinking water on the Somme front, and it donated £50 to provide 'comforts for drivers in the Army Service Corps in France and Belgium'. The donation appeared in a list published in the press, which included other vehicle manufacturers such as Daimler, Foden and Leyland, and a number of vehicle operators among which were Dennis customers Aldershot & District Traction and Thomas Tilling.

A number of Dennis employees joined the armed forces to fight in the Great War. For those still toiling in Guildford, where the factory was soon working round the clock to produce lorries, a letter from Lord Kitchener was designed to raise morale.

He wrote to the directors: 'I wish to impress upon those employed by your company the importance of the Government work upon which they are engaged. I fully appreciate the efforts which the employees are making, and the quality of work turned out. I trust that everything will be done to assist the military authorities by pushing on all orders as rapidly as possible. I should like all engaged by your company to know that it is fully recognised that they, in carrying out the great work of supplying munitions of war, are doing their duty for King and Country equally with those who have joined the Army for active service in the field.'

Dennis employees were issued with badges carrying the words 'Working on HM Service' inscribed around a Union Jack. The company's growth had created a housing shortage in Guildford and in 1916 it built 28 houses for its employees in Woking Road.

In the early days of the war the company was still building small numbers of vehicles for civilian use and for export. The latter included a 38hp tractor for South African Railways

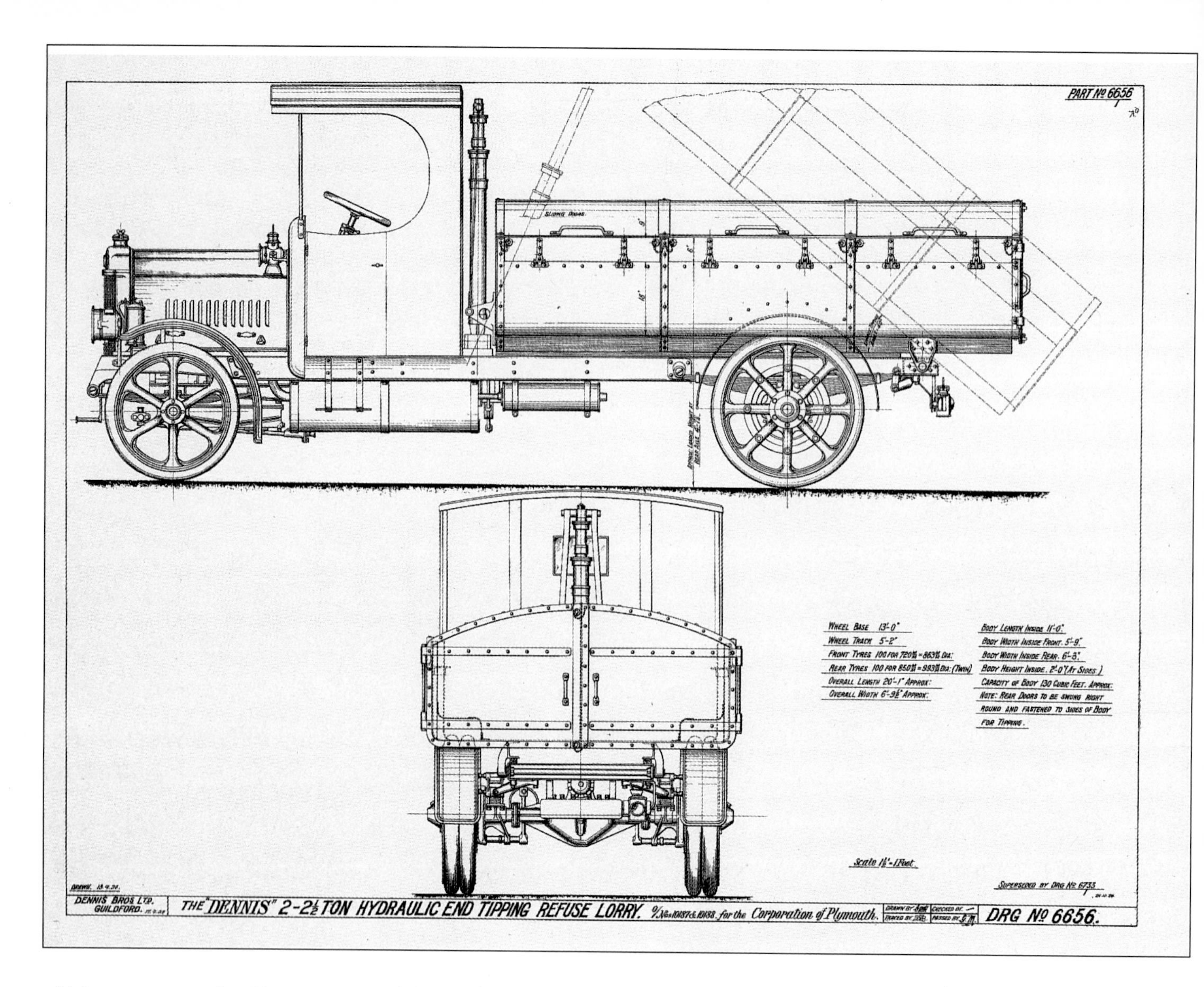

which was rear-engined to put more weight on the driving wheels, and which could pull loads of up to 9 tons at speeds of up to 12mph. It had a duplex induction system with two carburettors and was able to run on petrol or paraffin.

To conserve fuel, a few operators converted their Dennises to run on coal gas, stored in a bag on top of the vehicle. The Co-operative Wholesale Society in Manchester converted a 3-ton van, while Chapman of Eastbourne had a pre-war charabanc converted. Chapman, incidentally, had been a pioneer operator of touring holidays and in the summer of 1914 was running a Dennis charabanc on tours from Eastbourne to Llandudno and to Lands End. The Lands End tour covered 660 miles, a bold undertaking in the early days of motorised transport, but not an uncomfortable one according to Chapman who said: 'A lady of 70 expressed herself highly delighted at the tour and free from fatigue'.

Another alternative method of propulsion around this period was the petrol-electric, in which a petrol engine drove a generator which powered electric motors driving the rear wheels. The gas experiments had been done by Dennis customers, but the company itself took

> But — let the country-dweller beware of two things.
>
> If not within the working boundaries of a brigade, the strong possibility is that he will be destitute of aid when the fire-emergency suddenly arises. For the limits of each brigade are very clearly defined, and, failing a pre-arrangement whereby, for a certain annual sum, based usually upon rateable value, any given property is 'covered' for fire, the distracted owner may find himself helpless.
> *— from Dennis brochure promoting portable fire pumps*

Above:
Dennis was doing well with municipal sales in the 1920s. This refuse collector for Plymouth Corporation featured a hydraulic tipping ram so that the load could easily be dumped at the end of a days work.

a direct interest in the petrol-electric concept. W A Stevens of Maidstone was the chief proponent of the idea, best known in the Tilling-Stevens range of buses built before and after World War I. In 1916 Stevens Petrol Electric Vehicles entered into an agreement with Dennis to produce petrol-electric trucks and buses, and these were known as Dennis-Stevens. They were based on the subvention chassis, but with a larger-capacity radiator which carried the Stevens name.

The first buses to be operated by Cardiff Corporation were six Dennis-Stevens single-deckers delivered in 1920 and these were followed by six double-deckers in 1922, after which the Corporation switched to conventional petrol-engined Dennises, buying 78 by 1929 — and before ordering the first, considering the products of no fewer than 20 other chassis makers. But however well Dennis's petrol-engined buses were doing, the petrol-electrics were not a success and the project with Stevens was abandoned.

When the war had begun, Dennis's directors were worried that the country's diminishing stock of cart horses might tempt touring car manufacturers to have a go at building heavy vehicles. But when the war ended, the problems facing the company were rather different.

Firstly, there was a sudden drop in demand for lorries. Dennis, like those other lorry makers supplying the War Department, had been working night and day simply to satisfy the apparently insatiable needs of the war. At a stroke that business vanished.

Secondly, there was a vast fleet of lorries no longer needed by the military which would soon find their way back to Britain from the battlefields of Europe to be rebuilt

Above:
A more typical 30cwt lorry — a model which brought Dennis considerable sales success in the 1920s.
Peter Durham.

Right:
Low-loading versions of the 30cwt chassis with small wheels were built primarily for municipal work. This compactor refuse collector could be more easily loaded thanks to the lowered chassis. Rubbish was tipped in the opening at the front and pushed to the rear by a sliding bulkhead. The body tipped to unload.

and sold for civilian service, undermining sales of new lorries and buses.

And as if that was not enough, the company had a factory which ranked as one of the biggest lorry-building facilities in Europe, thanks in part to the investment in expansion which had taken place to satisfy the needs of the War Department. The company had the capacity to build somewhere around 2,500 vehicles a year. But if it did, where could they be sold?

Dennis was facing a challenge such as it had never faced before. Years of continued expansion in relatively easy trading conditions looked as though they were coming to a sudden end.

The company adopted a two-pronged attack. It developed new models, and it looked for new markets. The 3-ton subvention model had been a great success. It was improved, and joined by improved 4- and 5-ton models too. The company's capital was increased to £600,000 and the '1913' dropped from its title, making it plain Dennis Brothers Ltd once again.

The increase in capital allowed it to purchase its engine supplier, White and Poppe, in 1919. Dennis was W&P's biggest customer and both Alfred White and Peter Poppe joined the company's board. Engine production remained at Coventry — for the time being.

To cultivate new markets, Raymond Dennis embarked on an ambitious 60,000 mile world tour, gaining market intelligence while promoting the company's proven products. The record of the subvention lorries was there for all to see, underscoring any claims made about reliability and durability. The work of Dennis's fire engines was also well-known, and in 1917 one had been pumping continuously for 17 days in the great Salonika fire. A second had pumped for 10 days. These were impressive achievements. Sales catalogues were produced in French and Spanish, as the

Left:
A growing number of companies realised that motor vehicles had considerable promotional value. These included Lyons, which had this 30cwt model fitted out as a travelling shop, complete with loudspeaker, mounted above the cab.

Below:
In the period immediately after World War 1 bus chassis were still based on lorry designs, with a high straight frame and solid tyres. At this time buses were restricted to a leisurely 12mph.

Above:
In the mid-1920s the 4-ton chassis was a popular choice with a number of London bus operators. Most had solid tyres when new, but were later converted to pneumatics. This London example is seen passing Big Ben in 1973 with radio personality Dave Lee Travis alongside the driver.

company sought new markets.

In 1923 a London sales office was opened in Great Portland Street, then the centre of the motor trade. A separate company, Dennis-Portland Ltd, was formed and sold the 2½-ton goods chassis which was also available with a bus body. This design dated from 1919. Vehicles were badged Dennis Portland, but the idea was not a success and was soon dropped.

All of this effort to create more sales didn't save the company from having to cut its capacity. In the summer of 1920 around 140 workers were laid off, cutting the workforce to some 650. Pay was £4 a week with two weeks' notice. Plans for a factory extension were postponed.

In an effort to recover lost ground — and Dennis had not been as hard hit as some — the early 1920s saw diversification. Drawing on its experience with pumps, in 1921 the company launched a vacuum cesspool emptier. This could not only drain a cesspool into a tank mounted on the vehicle, but the pump could be reversed to discharge the contents at a sewage disposal site — though woe betide any driver who got it wrong! Local authorities were quick to order this revolutionary new vehicle, and Dennis laid the foundations of what was to become an enviable reputation in the field of specialist vehicles in an area that would later become known as public hygiene. Street-cleaning lorries soon followed.

In 1922 a very different product was announced: a motor lawn mower. It might have lacked the excitement of a fire appliance, or even the impressive size of a double-deck bus, but the Dennis mower helped keep the factory busy and found a steady stream of customers for the best part of 50 years. The mower was powered by a single-cylinder 600cc Dennis side-valve engine.

It wasn't as strange a diversification as it might sound. The company was already doing a lot of business with local authorities — and local authorities were responsible for many acres of public parks. The mowers were innovative too. Dennis was the first motor mower manufacturer to include a differential and a reverse gear. This allowed the mower to be reversed out of a corner without scuffing the grass. The mowers were solidly-built, weighing around 5cwt.

Always quick to sell benefits, the Dennis mower sales brochure claimed that one man equipped with a Dennis mower could do in 3½ hours a job that would take two men and a horse 7 hours, or two men without a horse 11 hours. The first motor mowers were available with a seat located above a grass roller. In 1925 a Dennis motor mower was supplied to Windsor Castle.

In 1922 Dennis was manufacturing its own pumps and offered these for fitment to other manufacturers' chassis — contemporary publicity showed a Dennis pump on a Ford Model T fire engine. The company also introduced trailer and portable pumps. A mid-1920s brochure listed some 500 users.

During 1923 sales were running well below the capacity of Dennis's factory. At the company's annual general meeting, chairman Nicholas Andrew commented drily: 'More than once the condition of our order book has caused our sales department much anxiety.' At the same time Raymond Dennis — now Sir

Raymond, following the granting of a KBE for services to the war effort — strongly attacked the government's *laissez faire* policy: 'By dumping American, as well as British, war-worn vehicles on our market and permitting the free importation of foreign-built commercial chassis, produced in enormous quantities for an unlimited and highly-protected market on the one hand and by lower paid labour based on depreciated currencies on the other, they have brought many firms to positions from which it is almost impossible to recover.'

Above:
The use of pneumatic tyres from the middle of the 1920s meant an instant improvement in ride quality and in vehicle handling, although a few years were to pass before the open charabanc was replaced by the totally-enclosed coach.

Left:
The E-type chassis featured a lower frame than previous lorry-based models and was the first forward-control bus in the Dennis model range. ***Michael Fowler.***

By the middle of the decade things were looking up. A new range of light 25cwt chassis was introduced in 1923 with a 2.7-litre petrol engine. It was described by Raymond Dennis as 'The first serious attempt of any British commercial vehicle manufacturer to meet, in price, the American and continental competition'. But at £295 it still only sold in small numbers, being undercut in price by models of a similar capacity from higher volume car-makers. Weights at this time, incidentally, referred to carrying capacity. It was only after World War 2 that it became more common to describe goods vehicles by their gross weight.

The 25cwt chassis was however the forerunner of an altogether more successful 30cwt model, keeping Dennis in a segment of the market which builders working with car-type components had trouble in tackling. This appeared in 1925 and used the same engine; two were delivered to the royal family for use at Buckingham Palace and Windsor Castle, earning Dennis the coveted Royal Warrant as suppliers to King George V. At the other end of the weight range a new 6-tonner chassis made its appearance in 1924.

The company was still doing well with buses and charabancs. In 1925 Greyhound of

We would point out that this new Lawn Mower has been designed and is now being manufactured by the well-known Engineering Firms of Dennis Bros., Ltd., of Guildford and White & Poppe, Ltd., of Coventry.

The Public is thereby assured of obtaining an article which will be superior in every respect to any similar Machine previously offered.

The fact that during the war these Firms jointly employed over 12,000 people on mechanical work of the utmost precision will give the public an idea of the size of their Factories, which are equipped with the finest automatic machinery, thus ensuring accuracy and inter-changeability.

— *from Motor Lawn Mower brochure*

Right:
A late 1920s EV for Vanguard, a South Wales operator.

Bristol introduced Britain's (some say the world's) first long-distance express coach service using a fleet of Dennis 4-tonners. This ran from Bristol to London, a distance of 125 miles. The 1920s saw remarkable and rapid advances in bus chassis design as Dennis and other lorry builders developed new models built specifically for passenger carrying. Tyre technology was advancing too, with the appearance of pneumatic tyres which gave better ride and roadholding than the solid tyres which had been fitted thus far.

The first London bus operator to get approval to run on pneumatic tyres, Admiral (a competitor for the altogether more famous General), did so in 1925 with a fleet of Dennis single-deckers. The Metropolitan Police, who exercised strict control over London's buses, had been concerned that in the event of a puncture a pneumatically-tyred bus might veer out of control with drastic consequences. Pneumatic tyres were not allowed on London double-deckers until 1928.

There had also been concern about the effects of four-wheel braking, but this too was accepted in London in 1926 — and again the first bus so fitted was a Dennis, also in the go-ahead Admiral fleet.

New models appeared in quick succession. The E-type bus chassis had a frame which was almost 7in lower than the previous lorry-based models which meant a lower floor line with fewer steps. The Dennis worm axle was changed so that the worm was beneath the axle rather than above it, which also contributed to the lower floor. The E was of forward-control layout for the first time on a Dennis, putting the driver alongside the engine rather than behind it, and giving more space for passengers. Pneumatic tyres were standard on this and all subsequent new models. A normal-control type, the F, was also available, but sold in smaller numbers. Both were powered by an updated version of the White and Poppe four-cylinder 6.24-litre petrol engine, rated at 70bhp at 1,700rpm.

Major buyers included the municipal transport operations in Accrington, Cardiff, Leeds, Lincoln, Nottingham, Portsmouth and Walsall. In Nottingham the corporation's bus fleet numbered 76 vehicles in 1928 and all but six were Dennises, including 26 new E-types. Municipal bus operation was introduced to Colchester in 1928 using Dennises; there were 19 on the road by the end of 1929 and they had been used to replace the town's tramway system. Company operators included South Wales Transport which ran 76 E- and EV-types; Yorkshire Woollen District Transport had 65.

After the E and F, came the G and H, both appearing in 1927. The G was a bus version of the 30cwt lorry chassis, powered by the same 36bhp side-valve 2.72-litre engine. It had a

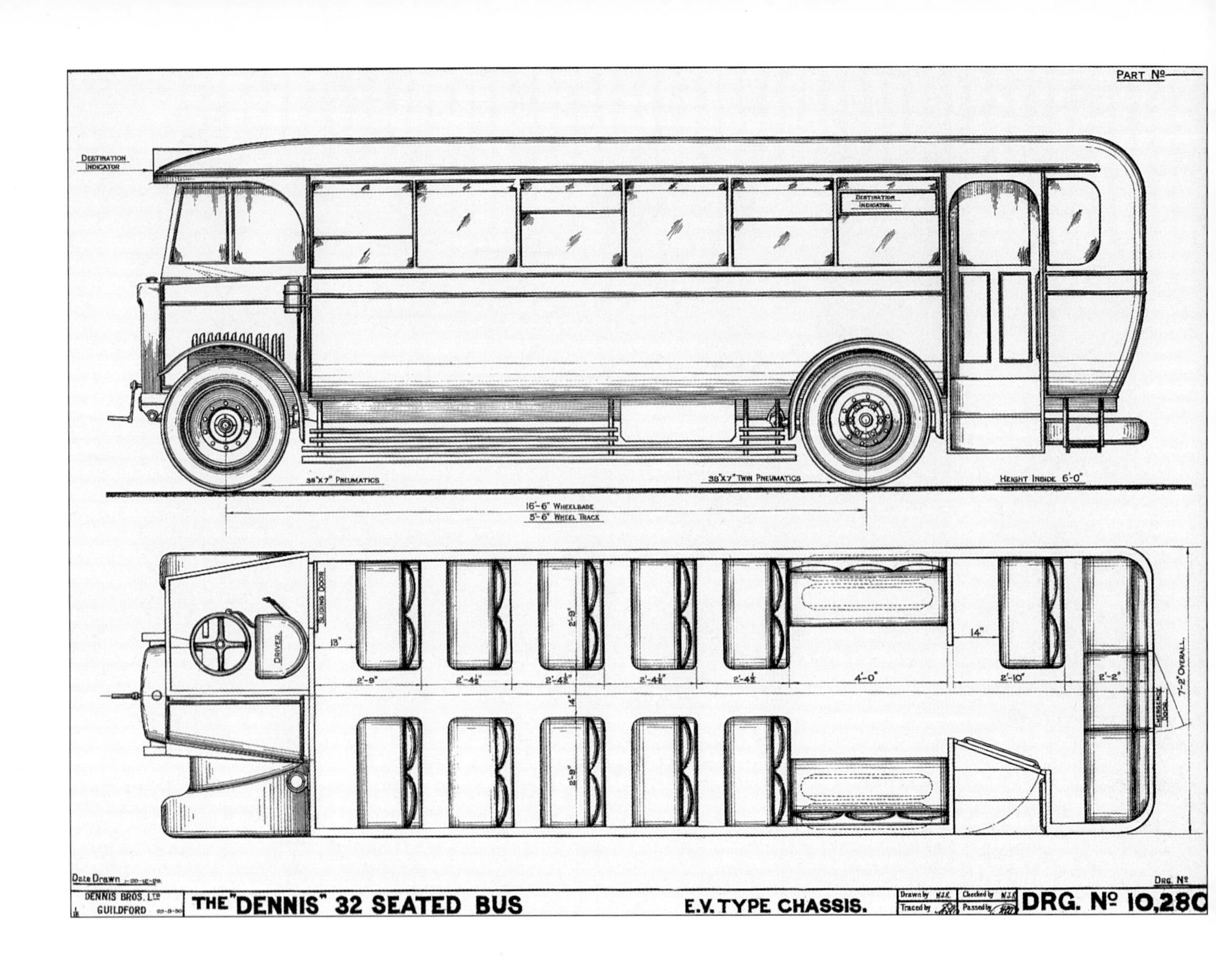

Above:
The EV was offered with Dennis built bodywork.

Left:
Aldershot & District was a customer for the new H-series low-frame double-deck version of the E-range.

Above:
Waiting for the whistle! It's the end of the day and the men are ready to go home. Many have bicycles and most are wearing caps — and a couple seem to have sneaked under the rope blocking the exit. An Aldershot & District bus leads a line of assorted commercial vehicles awaiting completion or ready for delivery.

dropped frame and longer springs to give a softer ride than the lorry and was designed to carry 20-seat bodywork. A slightly longer wheelbase was offered on the GL from 1929, which was powered by an overhead-valve variant of the 2.72-litre engine, producing 42bhp. A six-cylinder 70bhp engine option was added at the same time. Most Gs and GLs were sold to country bus operators. The 20-seat capacity was important, as the maximum then permitted for operation without a conductor.

Right:
Dennis has a long association with Hong Kong. This trio of four-tonners had dual-door bodywork and were for the Kai Tack Motor Bus Co.

The H was the first purpose-designed double-decker from Guildford, and was broadly similar to the single-deck E. It evolved as the HS, with improved engine mountings and servo-assisted braking, and then the HV with vacuum brakes. There was a corresponding EV single-decker. Buyers for the new double-decker

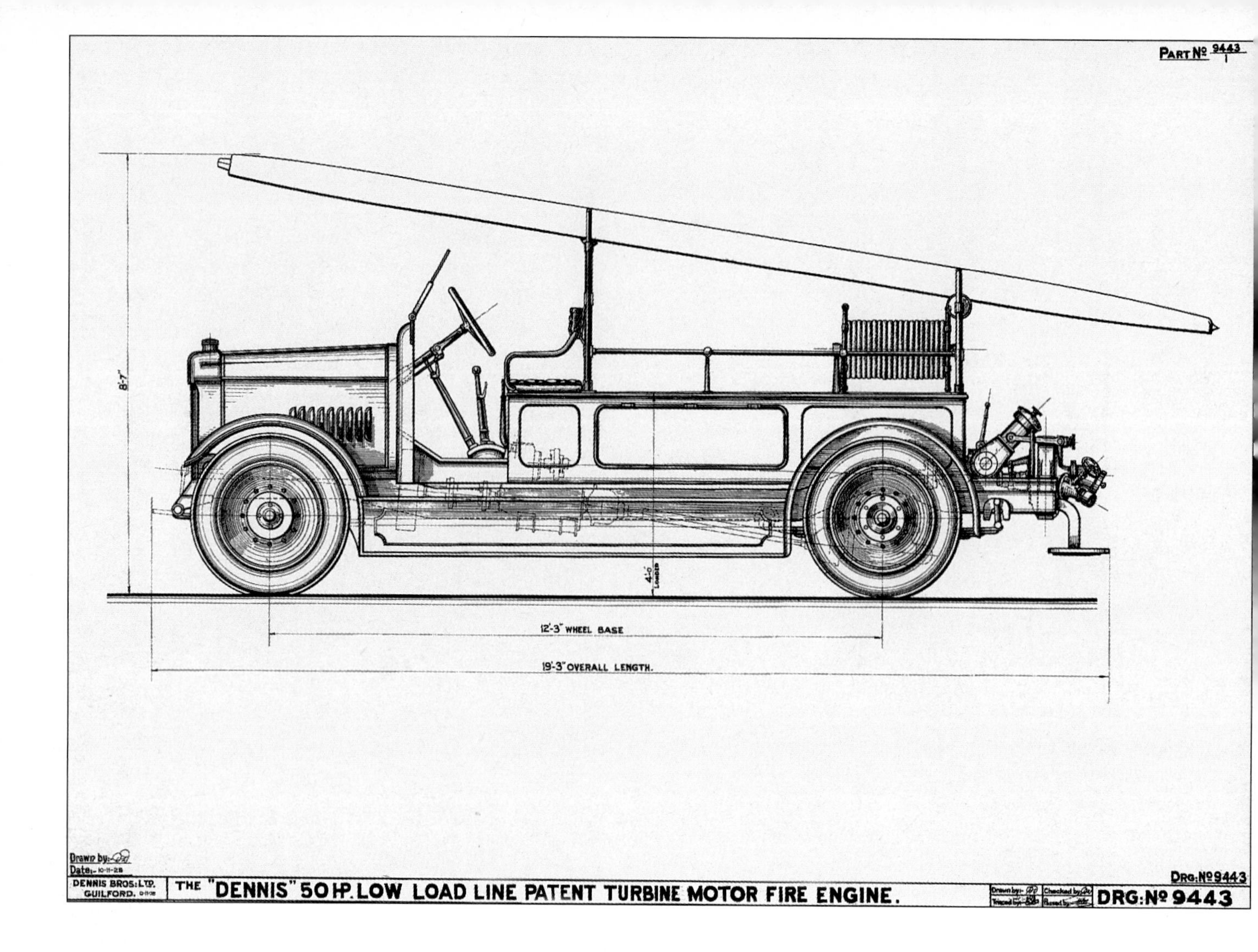

Above:
Fire sales were prospering. This is a 1928 drawing of a 50hp appliance.

included London General and Walsall corporation.

The E, F, G and H all had comparatively short lives, such was the pace of change in the late 1920s and early 1930s, and in retrospect can be seen as a step towards a modern bus generation. The frames were low, which was a major advance, but on the forward-control E and H models the driving position was still relatively far back, being just behind the front axle rather than above it, as would soon become the industry norm.

The last new model in the 1920s took Dennis into the big league, with its heaviest lorry chassis yet — 'Of gigantic strength, yet devoid of useless weight', to quote the sales brochure. This was a six-wheel 12-tonner, powered by a 6.13-litre 100bhp six-cylinder petrol engine. It was of forward-control design, had twin worm-drive axles and brought Dennis into an area which had hitherto been the preserve of manufacturers such as Leyland Motors. It was the right model, but at the wrong time. There was a major recession on the way — not that the management at Dennis could have foreseen it — and it was going to have a horrendous effect on British industry, cutting output and jobs. It was also going to have a serious effect on lorry sales. A six-wheel bus, the M-type, was on the drawing board at Guildford but did not enter production. A relaxation of the weight limits on two-axle buses had brought to an end a short-lived interest in six-wheelers.

Dennis had a broad product range — buses from 20-seaters to double-deckers, goods vehicles from 30cwt to 12 tons, plus fire engines, municipal vehicles and lawn mowers. But to meet the depressed 1930s there were more changes on the way.

> The Dennis subvention model was accepted by the War Department under its subsidy scheme as the result of arduous tests; and, furthermore, was accepted the first time it was submitted for trial, thus proving that in this, as in other products of our factory, every detail had been thoroughly worked out and tested before the vehicle was put into service.
>
> The Dennis subvention model is the finest chassis on the market for the carriage of useful loads up to 3½ tons in all parts of the world and on good and bad roads alike.
> — *from Dennis subsidy model brochure*

The 1930s

Difficult years

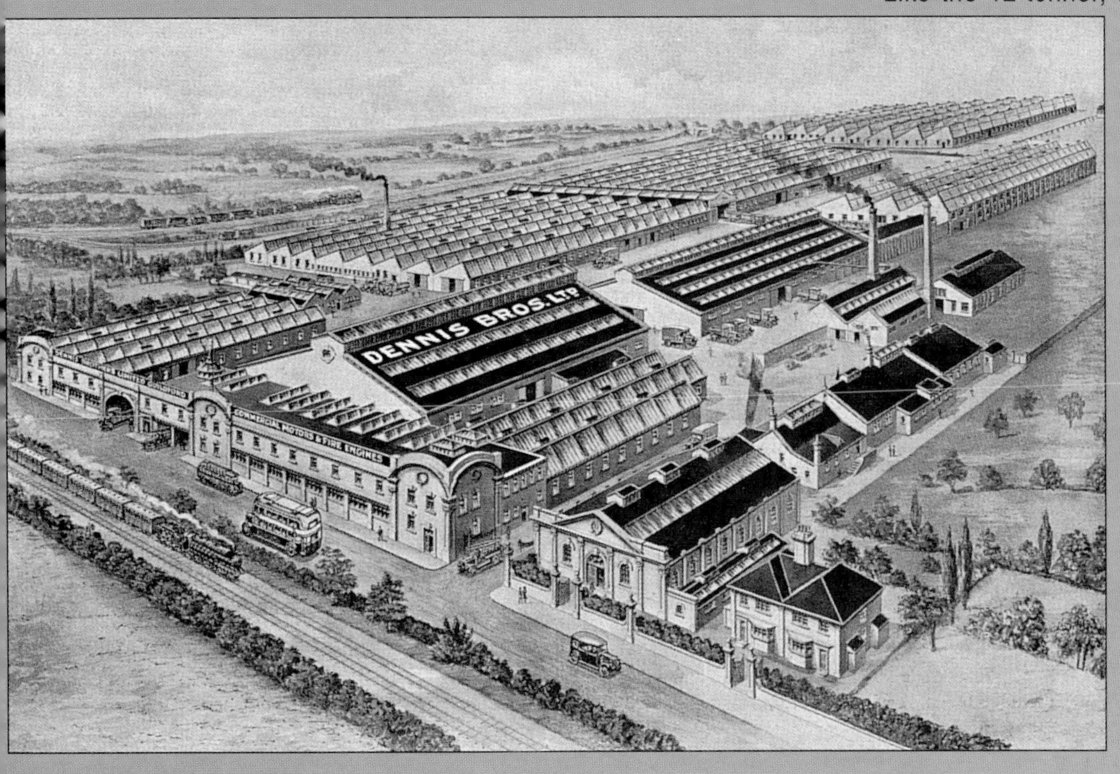

Above:
An artist's impression of the factory as it looked around 1930.

Right:
In 1931 Dennis delivered 108 lorries to the Great Western Railway. Seven two-tonners pose in Guildford prior to delivery.

wo new bus chassis appeared in 1930, just as the great depression of the inter-war years began to bite. One, the double-deck Lance, was set to continue in production for the rest of the decade. The other, the single-deck Arrow, was quickly replaced by the lower cost Lancet. The Arrow was designed to perform on the road; the Lancet was designed to sell in a difficult market.

The Arrow was powered by the six-cylinder ohv engine used in the 12-ton lorry. Like the 12-tonner, the Arrow had its four-speed gearbox mounted in unit with the engine. With 100bhp on tap — which was a lot in 1930 — the Arrow could in theory reach a breathtaking 56mph. The legal limit for buses and coaches in Britain was a stately 30. But this engineering came at a price — a shade over £1,000 — and 1930 was not the time to be selling on quality and performance. The market wanted economy. So while the Arrow remained available until 1934, fewer than 60 were sold.

The Lance was in effect a double-deck version of the Arrow, with the same 100bhp engine. This replaced the H-types and had a slightly lower frame and a proper forward-control driving position. A simplified version with a twin-plate clutch in place of the complex 14-plate type originally used, and with a revised frame, appeared in 1931. This improved model was known as the Lance II.

Dennis was quick to publicise customers for the Lance and in 1931 listed the municipalities of Accrington, Coventry, Doncaster, Dundee, Hull, Leeds and Salford. Accrington's first buses, in 1928, were half a dozen Dennises, but Dundee, although on the list, did not in fact become a Dennis bus buyer. Salford was running 43 Dennises by 1932, which included 31 double-deckers. London General bought 25 Lance IIs for its Overground fleet. The biggest Lance buyers in the 1930s were Walsall Corporation with 80,

Top Left:
A four-tonner disguised as a Daren loaf. Similar bodywork was fitted to a 12-tonner for Daren.

Left:
A six-ton chassis in use with a London firm of removers, complete with drawbar trailer.

and Aldershot & District with 50.

The Lance was briefly offered with the four-cylinder 85bhp petrol engine as the Lance Four. This cut £100 off the £1,095 selling price of the standard chassis — but no doubt cut a fair bit off the performance too.

Aware that economics were weighing heavily against the Arrow, Dennis lost no time in coming up with a lower-cost single-deck chassis, the Lancet, introducing a name which was to reappear later in the company's history. The Lancet was launched at the 1931 Commercial Motor Show in London. It had a twin-plate clutch, as featured on the Lance II, but was powered by a four-cylinder 5.7-litre petrol engine. The power unit might have been less refined than that of the Arrow, but with a selling price of £595 it was a sacrifice operators were willing to make. It soon found eager buyers, both large and small. One of the biggest users was the West Yorkshire Road Car Co, which took 80; the North Western

Above:
The Lance double-decker sold steadily throughout the 1930s, customers including London General's Overground operation. These had metal-framed bodies by Metro-Cammell at a time when most bus bodies were still timber-framed. This remarkable picture was made using just four buses. They were photographed at different points on the road and the resultant series of negatives was united in a single image to produce the impression of a convoy ready for delivery.

Road Car Co had 64. Other significant fleet orders came from South Wales Transport, with 70, and Belfast corporation.

Interest was growing in oil engines — as diesels were then known — as an alternative to petrol for heavy vehicle operation. Bus operators in particular could see advantages in lower fuel bills and greater durability. The directors at Dennis were watching developments and, with White and Poppe under their control, were planning ahead.

However development of a diesel engine in-house was to take a little time, not least because the decision had been made to close White and Poppe's Coventry factory (which was then sold to car manufacturer Triumph) and to transfer engine production to Guildford, along with the machine tools and those employees willing to relocate south. This happened in 1933. To provide housing for relocated White and Poppe employees Dennis built its own small housing estate on a 21 acre site in Guildford in 1934 — Dennisville.

To meet demands for oil-engined vehicles Dennis reached an agreement which gave the company exclusive rights to fit Armstrong-Saurer diesels in its bus chassis. A six-cylinder was offered in the Lance and a four-cylinder in the Lancet, but there were few takers. In any event, the agreement was short-lived, with the appearance in 1934 of the first Guildford-built oil engines.

The first was the Dennis Lanova 6.5-litre 82bhp four-cylinder unit which was not a great success and Dennis's engineers worked on an improved oil engine with four valves per cylinder. This, the 85bhp 6.5-litre O.4, was smooth, had plenty of torque, and quickly earned a reputation for reliability in service. The oil engine added £175 to the price of a chassis, making the Lancet £825 as against £650 with a petrol engine.

It was fitted in a revised Lancet II chassis, also offered with a 90bhp petrol engine. By standardising on four cylinders rather than six, Dennis was

> While it is in full possession of all the essential qualifications of a chassis designed for a 20-seat passenger body, it caters simultaneously for the high degree of luxury required by present-day usage, and for a very liberal proportion of the takings to be transmitted to the proprietor as profit.
> *— Dart brochure, 1930*

> As it is our distinction to have built motor vehicles for 42 years, we have seen more developments than most of our Operator-friends can — or care to — remember.
>
> We take pride in the knowledge that throughout this period, our products have contributed a large share to the success of road transport, and, to the utmost of our ability, we have ensured that the new Ajax shall be a further contribution, yours to employ and enjoy.
>
> — *Ajax brochure, 1937*

Below:
Walsall Corporation was a major Lance user in the 1930s.

able to shorten the bonnet of the Lancet II, thus increasing the space available for passengers. Up to 39 seats could be fitted to a Lancet II, compared with 35 in most of its competitors, offering operators a useful increase in earning capacity.

The O.4 engine was fitted to Lances for Walsall Corporation. However Dennis was not promoting this combination, believing that 80bhp was not really adequate for a fully-loaded double-decker, and was instead developing a six-cylinder version, which would produce 100bhp. This, the O.6, appeared in prototype form in 1939, but series production was halted by the outbreak of war. A small number of chassis were fitted with Gardner diesels in the 1930s.

On goods models the O.4 oil engine was fitted to the 7½-tonner from 1937 as an option to Dennis's 5.7-litre petrol unit and replacing the Gardner 6LW which had previously been offered. The 7½-ton model had been introduced in 1934.

Britain had a somewhat ambivalent attitiude towards trolleybuses, although the 1930s saw considerable expansion of trolleybus operation in a number of towns and cities throughout the country. This ambivalence was shared by Dennis, who in the mid-1930s kept its options open by including a trolleybus on its model lists, but without any specification details. These could be had, said the company's publicity coyly, 'on application'. Had any Dennis customer wanted a trollleybus the Lance chassis could have been used; but none did. However, in an ironic twist, the very last trolleybus to be built in Britain was a Dennis — but that was still some 50 years off.

The depressed early 1930s had seen Dennis focus its attention on passenger vehicles. Bus and coach travel was still growing, offering for many a cheap and fast alternative to rail. There was also growing pressure to abandon inflexible and expensive urban tramways and replace them with inexpensive motor buses. So it was a healthy market, with growth in the UK and some export business too. Dennis supplied bus chassis in the 1930s to Australia, South Africa and Brazil.

By contrast, road haulage was struggling. The road network was a long way from being able to cope efficiently with long-distance traffic — some might say little has changed — and whatever the inefficiencies of the railway companies, there were goods sidings in all major factories and bustling goods terminals in and around every town and city of any size.

Dennis continued to build lorries throughout the decade, but concentrated on municipal vehicles and fire engines. But here too, developments were closely tied in with new bus models.

The lightweight four-cylinder G-type bus had been replaced by the six-cylinder Dart —

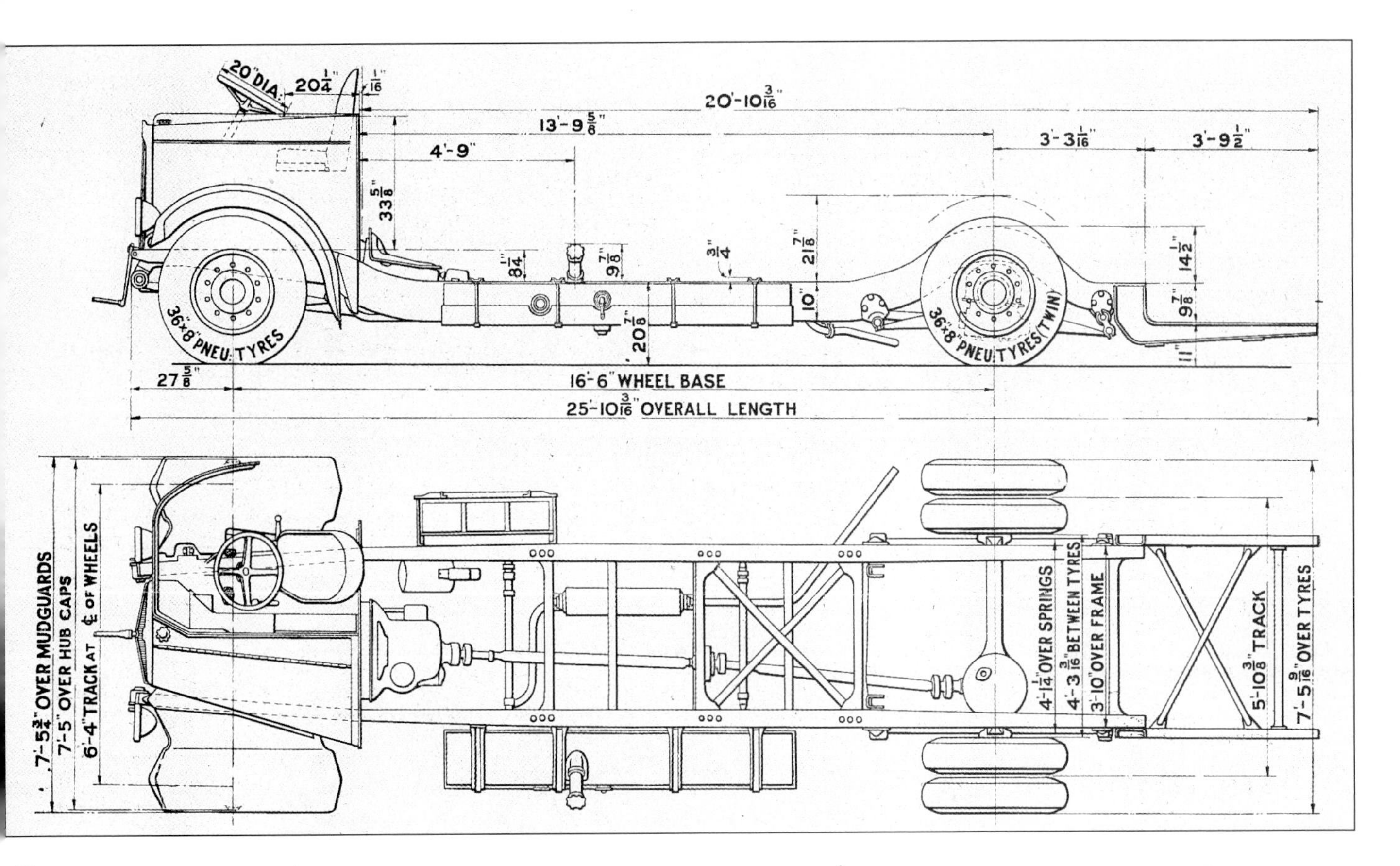

Above:
The Lance chassis

'nimble as a swallow', according to Dennis publicity — in 1929, transforming its performance with an increase in horsepower approaching 100 per cent — up from 36 to 70bhp. London General bought 42 Darts.

In 1933 a new light range appeared, available either as a 40/45cwt lorry or as the basis of a 20-seat bus called the Ace. The normal-control chassis had the front axle set back which made the new range highly manoeuvrable and gave it a particularly distinctive appearance with the radiator extending well forward of the wheels like a small snout. The nickname 'flying pig' was soon coined for this popular range. Power came from a new 60bhp 3.77-litre four-cylinder petrol engine. Some were built with Gardner 4LK oil engines, including 20 for use in rural East Anglia by the Eastern Counties Omnibus Co.

It was an instant success both as a bus and a lorry and was also available as a forward-control model, primarily for haulage use. A single-tyred trailing axle could be fitted to the goods versions to increase capacity to 3½ tons. Heavier loads could be carried by adapting the 40/45cwt chassis-cab to run as the tractive unit in a 6-ton articulated outfit.

Specialist applications for the new range included fire engines and assorted municipal vehicles, one of which, the Pactum, built on the company's growing strength in refuse collection. This could compress household rubbish, enabling lighter weight items such as empty tin cans to be squashed so that they took up less space. Consequently the amount of refuse which could be carried was increased, providing greater operating efficiency. Over 5,500 40/45cwt lorries and Ace buses were sold.

These models were soon joined by the broadly similar 50cwt and Mace forward-control types. These had the same driveline but uprated springs and bigger tyres.

Continuing the theme of parallel

> Dennis machines have never had the reputation of being 'Dead in three years' and the present models are no exception. Parts are bound to wear in time — but oversize dimensions and advanced metallurgy have set new standards for that — and spares are always available.
>
> There are many Dennis lorries still giving profitable service after 15 years' hard work, and a 10 years' life is no cause for comment. Thus do the accepted ideas of depreciation evaporate!
>
> — *40/45cwt brochure, 1937*

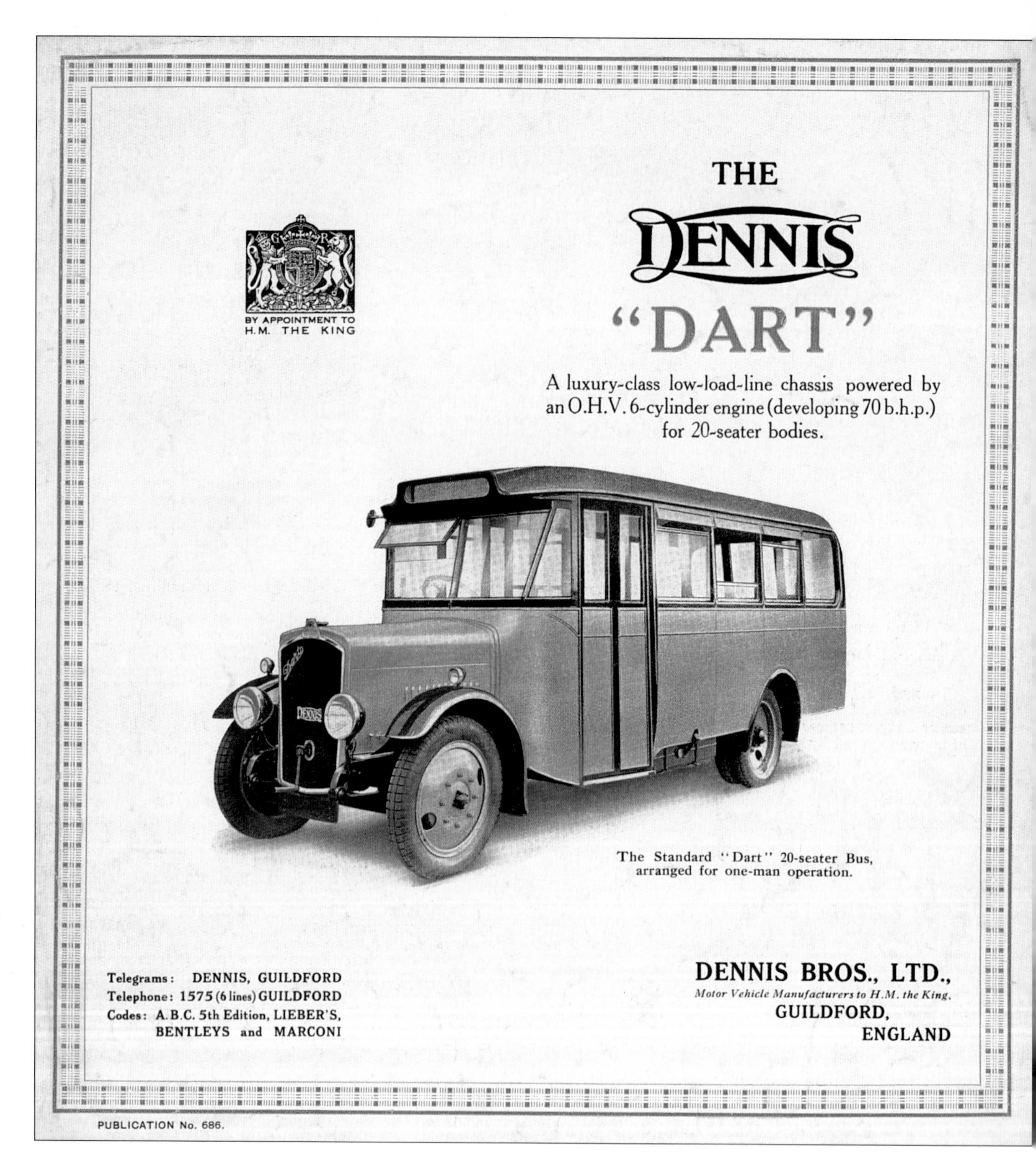

Above:
Dart brochure.

development of goods and light duty bus chassis, the normal-control 4-ton lorry of 1935 was soon followed by the Arrow Minor coach chassis which had different springs. The lorry sold well with 436 leaving the factory by 1940; the coach less so, with a mere 45 sales. Development on the 40/45cwt chassis saw the appearance of the Ajax lorry and companion Pike bus chassis. Total sales of both types was not much over 100.

There was one final spurt of model development in the late 1930s before the signs of another major war approaching in Europe brought new model plans to a standstill. In 1938 the light bus and coach range was rationalised. The new Falcon chassis inherited the driveline of the old Ace, Mace and Arrow Minor, had a relatively low frame, and two wheelbases to accommodate bodywork of between 20 and 32 seats. It came with the option of diesel power from Gardner (the 4LK) or Perkins (the P6). Fewer than 50 were built before the needs of wartime Britain brought production to a halt.

Above:
The Dart was built primarily for use as a small bus, but the Guildford branch of the St John Ambulance Brigade had one bodied as an ambulance. Note the spare wheel mounted on the body side and the bells above the front bumper.

The Dennis range of light trucks was wide with both normal-and forward-control models spanning the 40cwt to 5 ton weight range. Little development work had been done on heavier vehicles in the mid-1930s, partly because of the absence of a suitable oil engine. That changed in 1937 with the appearance at the Commercial Motor Show of the Max, a 6/8-tonner (12 tons gross) which used the O.4 diesel, or a newly-developed 6.8-litre 95bhp Big Four petrol. The final new model was a 5-tonner filling a gap in the range. This appeared in 1939 and was designed to meet the British regulations which allowed a

Right:
The goods version of the Dart, the two-tonner

Above:
The new Lancet single-deck chassis was introduced in 1931. By this time the charabanc had been rendered obsolete by a new generation of coaches which offered all-weather protection.

Left:
Over the years a good number of breweries used Dennis lorries to deliver their products. Hodgsons' Brewery was based at Kingston, not far from the Dennis factory.

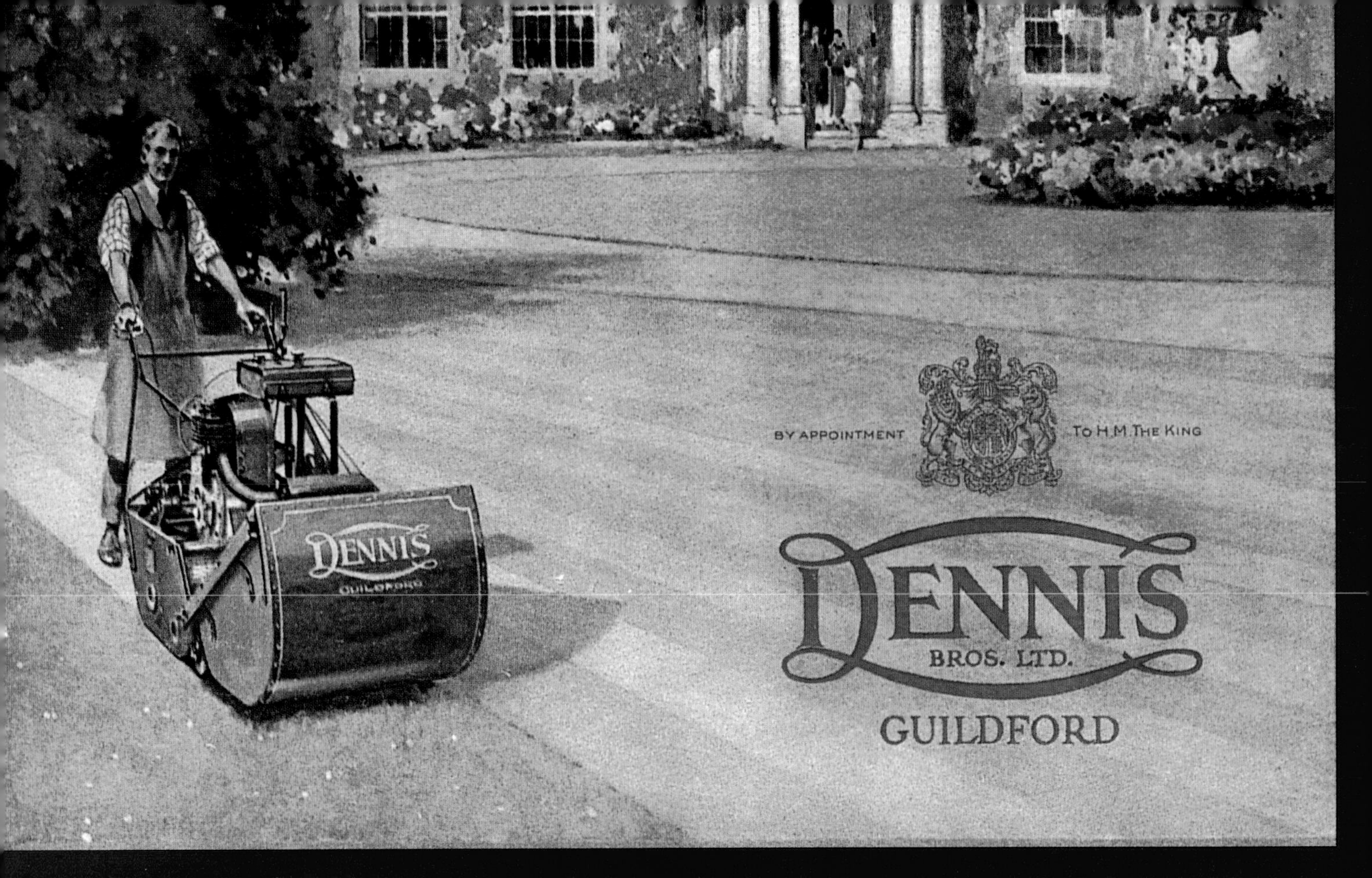

Above:
Lawn mower production continued throughout the 1930s. This is the cover of a brochure produced in 1933.

Right:
At the top of the weight range was the 12-ton six-wheeler, seen here as a milk tanker. It had a 100bhp six-cylinder petrol engine.

The Dennis 'Max' chassis means business, in both senses of the phrase. In appearance it is obviously of great strength and designed for carrying the 'Max'-imum loads permitted to a 4-wheeler. From the point of view of performance, it represents 'Max'-imum economy. Not only is it capable of carrying loads of 6-8 tons, dependent upon the type of body employed, but, with a 4-wheel trailer, an additional 8 tons may be conveyed, as nearly 100 B.H.P. is available.
— *Max brochure, 1938*

Left:
The Caledonian Omnibus Company was a major user of the Lancet and by the end of the 1930s had 34 in service. This is a 1936 Lancet II.
Charles F. Klapper.

lorry of under 2½ tons unladen weight to run at 30mph. It was produced in both forward-and normal-control layouts with power coming from Dennis's 3.8-litre petrol engine. A diesel option was available, with the choice of Gardner 4LK or Perkins P6 engines. This was built in small numbers during the war — and emerged in 1945 as the appropriately-named Pax, the Latin for peace.

Dennis had coped well with the difficulties of the 1930s. It was exporting. It was selling reasonable numbers of buses. And its light

Left:
Bodywork being lowered onto an Arrow Minor chassis, destined for an overseas customer.

Left:
The lightweight 40/45cwt chassis was suitable for a wide variety of operations — lorries, vans, municipal vehicles, buses and coaches. Brighton Corporation used this 1935 example to maintain the overhead electric wires which powered its tram and trolleybus systems.
Peter Durham.

If unaccustomed to the activity of a big motor factory, the visitor to the Woodbridge establishment is likely to be confused by the continuous whine of high-speed machine tools, the groan and judder of a heavy 'rough' cut, the shriek of a cast iron component, the seismic tremor from a power hammer, or the impenetrable staccato of a riveting machine. To the habitue, however, the noise and bustle is of little consequence. He is able to recognise and appreciate the value of the production scheme, based upon the control of every individual machine and the efforts of every individual worker in order to serve as tributaries feeding the main stream — the chassis assembly line.
— *from* Why Dennis — and how, *1945*

truck range was doing very well, despite growing competition both from heavy lorry makers such as Leyland and from high-volume light vehicle builders such as Bedford. Fire sales too were going well, with over 100 units a year being supplied to brigades throughout Britain and overseas. A milestone in 1937 was the delivery of the 250th Dennis fire engine to the London Fire Brigade.

The 1930s ended on a sad note. In May 1938 Sir Raymond Dennis died, aged only 59. His brother John died just three months later. He was 67. This put great pressure on chairman Nicholas Andrews, and on Reginald Downing who, having been a director since 1913, was made joint managing director in

Right:
The 40/45cwt was known as the Ace when supplied for bus or coach use. Liverpool Corporation bought this Ace in 1935. It was used on a service to the airport, until the outbreak of World War 2 brought an end to most civilian flying. The streamlined body was designed to match the modernity of air travel.

Right:
Special bodywork an a 50cwt to promote CWS paints.

1939. He shared the managing directorship with William Fish, who had been on the board since 1928.

The changes at the top came as even more change was about to be forced on the company — as Britain declared war on Germany in September 1939.

Left:
The main chassis production line in the 1930s — the two left-hand lines are producing Lancets while the right-hand line is dedicated to the popular 40/45cwt models.

Below:
Fire brigades continued to be major customers for a wide range of Dennis products. This is a 1934 Braidwood Big Four. ***Roger Pennington.***

Right:
The Big Four was also exported — as shown by an example destined for Hong Kong.

Below:
Same year, different concept: Watford's Light Four fire engine had an enclosed cab.

Every vehicle that leaves these Works carries with it our reputation, bearing it to all parts of the country and overseas. For good or ill, it is our constant advertisement, seen by tens of thousands. We guard our reputation jealously, and our advertisement, if right, is invaluable. These elementary considerations, apart from any others, form an Unwritten Guarantee of our unstinted endeavour to secure perfection in every detail.
— 7/7½ton brochure, 1934

Above:
There was more to fire-fighting than high-profile fire engines. London Fire Brigade crews get a welcome cup of tea at a mobile refreshment van based on a 40/45cwt chassis.

Below:
A 45cwt chassis with Dennis bodywork.

Right:
The bonnetted version of the 40/45cwt chassis was as versatile as the forward-control type. A tractor unit is seen on test in Guildford. Articulated lorries of this type were operated by railway companies and breweries.

Right:
A side-tipper based on the neat 40/45cwt chassis at work on new housing in Guildford.

Right:
Street cleaners and gulley emptiers were a Dennis speciality. The flexible 40/45cwt was chosen for this duty by Tottenham in 1936. The cab has no nearside door, allowing the crew to jump in and out more easily in the days before stringent safety standards. A narrow-width version was offered for use in areas with restricted access.

Above:
Many brigades continued to specify traditional brass fittings. A Light Six pump escape delivered to Reading in 1938 has brass bell and brass trim on the headlamps and radiator shell. *Roger Pennington.*

The passenger, with his penny ticket or his 15-guinea tour-booking, is the man on whose opinion the operator really depends. What then are his reactions to the Falcon? His sense of sight is at once gratified; however little he knows of its craftsmanship, he realises — maybe subconsciously, but nevertheless he realises — that it is a capable-looking, attractive-looking vehicle.

He gets in and sits down, thankful for the absence of constriction, and appreciative of upholstery that receives and accommodates, but is nowhere obtrusive; should the road be, to his previous knowledge, bad, in the Falcon he will believe speedy repairs to have been made, for the rear springs, 60 ins. long, are the outcome of special investigations into comfort-riding, and the effectiveness is remarkable. Their oscillation-period under average loading has been determined at a frequency familiar to the human body; it corresponds with that of walking.

— *Falcon brochure, 1938*

World War 2

Boom, but out-gunned in the peace

controlled by the Ministry of Supply. This brought to a halt the output of Lances, Lancets and Falcons — although a few Lancets were allowed to be completed during the early years of the war to use up stocks of parts already in the factory. Some were allocated to Scottish operators — namely Caledonian and SMT. Although Caledonian had a number of Lancets in operation, Scotland was not an area where Dennis had sold many buses.

Right:
During World War 2 much of Dennis's production was turned over to supporting the war effort. However, small numbers of lorries were still being built. Wartime vehicles had more angular cabs. This lorry is delivering three trailer pumps — one being towed and two being carried. The trailing third axle was an unusual fitting and raised the 40/45cwt model's load capacity to 3½tons.

World War 1 had been a tough testing ground for vehicles. When it started in 1914, the motor lorry was in its infancy. Quarter of a century later designs had advanced with remarkable speed and motorised transport was going to play a key part both in defence and attack in World War 2 .

Aware of the importance of the production capacity of what was becoming one of Britain's major industries, the government laid down just who could build what amongst vehicle manufacturers. Bus production was to be the province of Daimler and Guy — and the allocation of buses to operators was tightly

Production of lorries for civilian use was halted, not only for Dennis, but for other makers too — except where a haulier could prove an urgent need for a vehicle. But where some vehicle manufacturers were switched solely to the production of military components, Dennis was allowed to build lorries for the War Office, which ordered 3,000 Max and 1,500 3-tonners. To cut costs and conserve materials these were built with angular utilitarian cabs, and the same no-frills cabs were fitted to the few allocated to haulage companies.

The factory was also building trailer pumps for fire-fighting — no fewer than 7,000 of them — along with a wide range of military equipment including the assembly of Churchill tanks using components supplied by other companies. In four years the company put

Left:
A utility cab being fitted to a Max chassis.

together 700 tanks and they were a common sight rumbling through the streets around the factory.

The body shop was also switched to military production, building bodies on Bedfords for the army. Add to all this some 3,000 tracked armoured personnel carriers plus tank gearboxes and bomb assemblies and you get some idea of the hive of activity which the Woodbridge works had become. Once again the factory was working 24 hours a day, and its engineering expertise was being used to the full.

Britain's motor industry was a prime target for Hitler's Luftwaffe — hence the heavy bombing on Coventry — and no time was wasted in applying camouflage paint to the huge Dennis works, located in a conspicuous position between the main A3 road to the south coast and the Southern Railway's lines. Being well away from other centres of car and lorry production must have worked in Dennis's favour. Guildford was a target for few enemy bombs; none hit the works.

In its latest form, the front end of the Max, with the curved dash and radiator-grille, presents a particularly attractive outline that readily blends with body-work of the finest class. The result is not only an easy-clean surface, but also the distinguished appearance appropriate to the vehicle of a judicious operator.
— Max brochure, 1946

> While passengers do not always analyse and express their reactions to travel-comfort, sub-conscious impressions are unavoidable. Those evoked by the Lancet III, with its easy, loping gait on the level, its assured mastery of hills, its absence of detonation and vibration, result in a goodwill that is reflected with increasing clarity in the operator's balance sheet...
> — *Lancet III brochure 1946*

The workforce doubled to cope with this unprecedented demand. Soon there were almost 3,000 people in Dennis's employ, confirming its position as Guildford's key employer.

By early 1945 it was clear that victory was in sight and the war would soon be over. As military production began to wind down, the management at Dennis looked ahead and tried to gauge the best course of action to keep the factory busy when peace returned. The company had a new six-cylinder diesel engine ready — the O.6. And it had a modern range of chassis which would see it through the early

Right:
Light armoured vehicles formed a major part of the Dennis war effort.

Right:
A normal-control Pax seen in operation with Fremlins, the brewer.

Top:
The Pax was also offered with forward control. ***Peter Durham.***

Left:
A rather fine brewery tanker in the shape of a Horla pulling a beer barrel trailer.

postwar period.

On buses and coaches things went fairly well — but on lorries the picture was not so bright with wholesale nationalisation of road haulage high on the political agenda. A new chairman was appointed who had a bus industry background, Sydney Garcke from the British Electric Traction group. He succeeded Nicholas Andrew, who remained a board member.

The end of hostilities saw a boom in Britain's bus and coach businesses. Suddenly freed from travel restrictions and the pressures of war, people wanted to go places. Private car ownership was low, so most journeys for work or pleasure had to be made by public transport. Factories throughout Britain were working flat out as the country embarked on a major drive to export, which in turn meant long waiting lists for those who could afford to buy a car, further helping public transport operators.

There were two key models in the postwar Dennis bus range — the double-deck Lance and the single-deck Lancet. The first postwar Lances took to the road in 1947, running for Lancashire United Transport.

> Limousine comfort is accorded to the driver by Dennis-designed steering and the 5-speed gearbox. The latter is arranged to provide a preselective overdrive which, by its simplicity of operation, encourages maximum fuel economy, and gives a steady cruising speed of 40-50 m.p.h.
> — *Lancet IV brochure, 1948*

Top:
Most Horlas had rather less exciting trailers. A hard-worked example is seen on duty at Liverpool docks. ***Peter Davies.***

Right:
A bonnetted Pax.

The last entered service in 1954 with Aldershot & District, Dennis's loyal local bus operator. Production was modest — 100 chassis for seven operators, with Aldershot & District being far and away the biggest user, with 72.

The Lance was offered with five- and six-cylinder Gardner engines, or with the new Dennis O.6 diesel. The O.6 was an efficient engine, producing a respectable 100bhp from 7.6 litres — by comparison Gardner's 6LW produced 102bhp from 8.4 litres. At a time when most bus chassis had four-speed gearboxes, the Lance was unusual in having a five-speed gearbox as an option. What it didn't have was the choice of a semi-automatic or preselector gearbox, and this may have contributed to its lack of sales among urban fleets, where an easy-to-drive fluid transmission was quickly becoming the norm as drivers faced growing traffic congestion.

Lancet production was quicker off the mark, and sales were much higher, totalling somewhere over 900 by 1951. A prototype of what was to become the Lancet III was in service with Aldershot & District in 1945. It was broadly similar to the prewar Lancet II, but with a longer bonnet to house the bigger O.6 engine. Aldershot & District took 143 Lancet IIIs, while

Top:
An early postwar Jubilant six-wheeler with the new cab introduced at the end of 1945. Its gently curved front profile was in stark contrast to the angular designs still being used by many other manufacturers.

From the well-tried stock of the pre-war Dennis 5-ton chassis, progressively improved under Active Service conditions, springs the new 'Pax' 5-tonner, new in strength, new in accessibility, new in ease of control and other refinements, but old in dependability, road-worthiness and economy...

The comfort of the driver has been closely studied in the relative positioning of seat, floor and controls. Neglect of a really comfortable seating position, combined with inadequate command of wheel, levers and pedals, has, in the past, placed an unnecessary strain on the drivers of many vehicles, but the benefits of the almost horizontal travel of the brake-pedal, which is situated not far below the level of the seat, and the 'organ'-type accelerator can only be appreciated by the physical experience of handling the Dennis 'Pax'.

— *Pax brochure, 1947*

other big users included the East Kent Road Car with 98 and Yorkshire Traction with 30.

Large numbers of Lancets sold to small coach operators — most Lancets were coaches rather than buses. A very small number were bodied in Dennis's own workshops but most were fitted with proprietary coachwork. Yeates of Loughborough, who were Dennis dealers, set up their own coach-building operation and fitted bodywork to some 80 Lancets. A small number were bodied by the Dennis dealer in South Wales, D J Davies.

There was also some export business. Lancets found their way to Australia, Madeira, South America (with left hand drive) and Trinidad. But the numbers were fairly small — under 100 in total. Long-wheelbase export models were marketed as the Lancet IV.

The O.6 engine was featured in the first new postwar goods vehicle, the Jubilant six-wheeler. This attractive 19-tonner (12 ton payload) featured a modern cab with a gently-curved front profile; a bonnetted version was launched at the International Trade Fair in Barcelona. Similar smoothly-styled cabs, but of different sizes, were used across the postwar range and set Dennis apart from most of its competitors who still used angular cabs of obvious prewar design. A short wheelbase

Left:
The four-wheel Max shared the Jubilant's cab. ***Peter Durham.***

Above:
The new cab was used on a stylish range of fire appliances. A 1956 F8 water tender illustrates a classic Dennis design.
Roger Pennington.

Top:
A Max and a Jubilant parade through Guildford. The occasion is not known, but the crowd is quite remarkable.

Left:
From a Spanish language Max brochure.

Top:
A Horla and a Max head a line of vehicles leaving the factory for a trade show in Barcelona.

Left:
Dennis quickly re-established its leading position in the refuse collection business after the war. These Paxits were in Hampstead, North London

Jubilant was available for tipper operators.

To cater for the tractive unit market a Jubilant derivative branded as the Dragon was on the Dennis stand at the 1948 Commercial Motor Show in London, designed to run at up to 20 tons gross. But by the time production began in the following year it had been renamed the Max 6 and was part of a family of six-cylinder Max lorries, built alongside the existing four-cylinder range. Max production ceased in 1956, to be replaced by the Hefty which used Dennis's biggest engine, the 120bhp 8-litre.

The lighter Pax model, offered in both normal- and forward-control versions, was in effect an updated version of the prewar 3- to 5-ton models. And, as the company started to develop a bewildering range of models and model names, the normal-control Pax was made available as a tractive unit and christened the Horla — a play on the southern English pronunciation of hauler — for this role. The Pax sold strongly to municipal fleets. Refuse collection vehicles were a significant part of this business. Engine choices were Dennis 3.8-litre 70bhp side-valve petrol or Perkins P6 diesel. Later Pax and Horla models had the option of the higher-powered (80bhp) overhead valve Dennis petrol unit.

Dennis claimed that two men could remove the cab from the forward-control Pax in less than 30 minutes, allowing for complete removal of the engine in less than an hour.

Adaptations of the Pax range saw the appearance in 1947 of a high-roof cab which was designed to match the contours of a new refuse collection body with a hydraulic ram to compress its contents. This became known as the Paxit and, later, the bigger Paxit Major.

A few bonetted Pax chassis were bodied as small buses in the late 1940s, pending the reintroduction of the Falcon, offered with the choice of Dennis petrol or Gardner 4LK diesel engines. When built with forward-control the Falcon was provided with a full-width scuttle which maintained the stylish curvature seen on the Dennis truck range. Major Falcon users in postwar days were East Kent with 15, and

Top right:
A plan of the factory at its peak in the early postwar years when production — including lawnmowers — was averaging 2,000 units annually.

Right:
This aerial view shows the factory as it was from the mid-1940s to the early 1970s. The main A3 road to Portsmouth snakes past on the right.

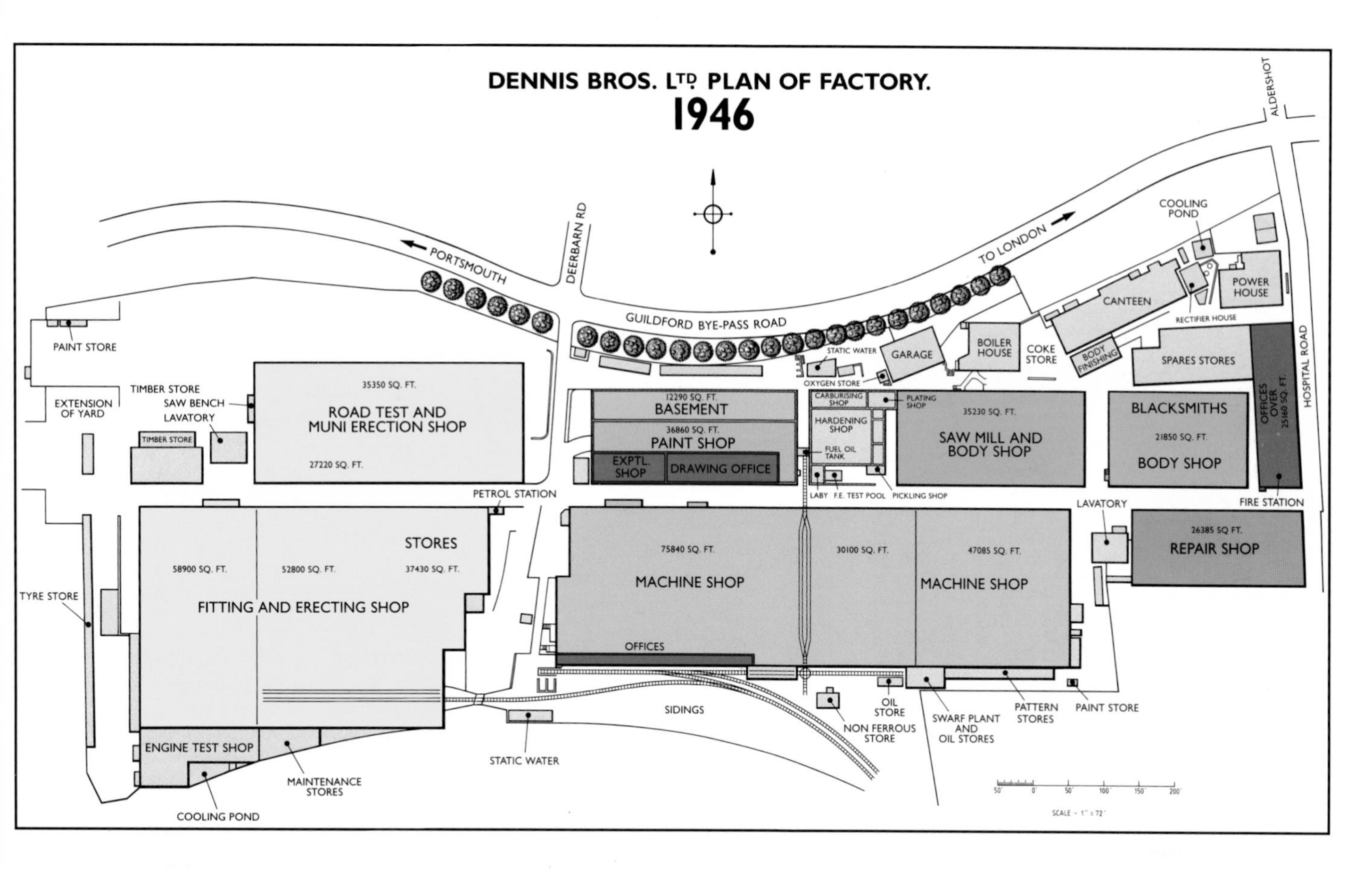

Aldershot & District with 30 — all normal-control models.

Lawn mower production was resumed after the war and in a 1947 brochure there was a list of customers. This started off with King George V and King George VI, included Queen Marie of Jugo-Slavia, three maharajahs, six dukes, three marquesses, 12

When reviewed against the many vehicles offered today, the Max represents an indisputably sound investment; the material strength, and substantial construction shown throughout in the specification are such to be physically capable of withstanding the stress of continued hard work.

In the general layout, and in the design of individual components, well-tried methods have been employed, methods which are completely familiar to operators, drivers and engineers everywhere. Yet the Max has little in common with mass-produced contemporaries.

The Max is designed against the need for a vehicle of moderate speed, to operate economically at up to 12 tons gross, and it is the long term economics of the Max that count. Long periods without major overhaul — long periods of consistent performance — in other words, long periods of profitable ownership.

— *Max brochure, 1951*

Above:
The Lancet was a best-seller in the late 1940s. Most went to small coach operators such as Safeway, a Somerset-based company.
Roger Pennington.

earls, two viscounts, 13 lords, two bishops, a host of educational and sporting establishments (including 14 golf clubs) along with Denham Studios, Schweppes and Lever Bros.

While lorry production was to continue to play a part at Guildford for another 25 years or so, Dennis struggled to find sales among the fleet operators. Road haulage nationalisation took effect from 1947, creating British Road Services and robbing Dennis of a large number of potential customers, as centralised buying became the order of the day. No big orders came the company's way.

The company's postwar production peak came in 1949, with output of 1,598 vehicles made up of 1,096 buses and trucks, 445

Left:
Aldershot & District remained a loyal customer. This is a Lance III of 1949 supplied to the operator.

Right:
Timber-framed bodywork was still the order of the day for buses and coaches. A part-completed Lancet is pictured outside the factory.

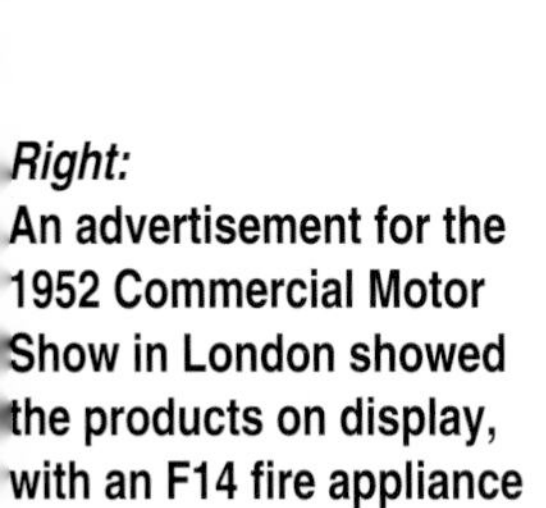

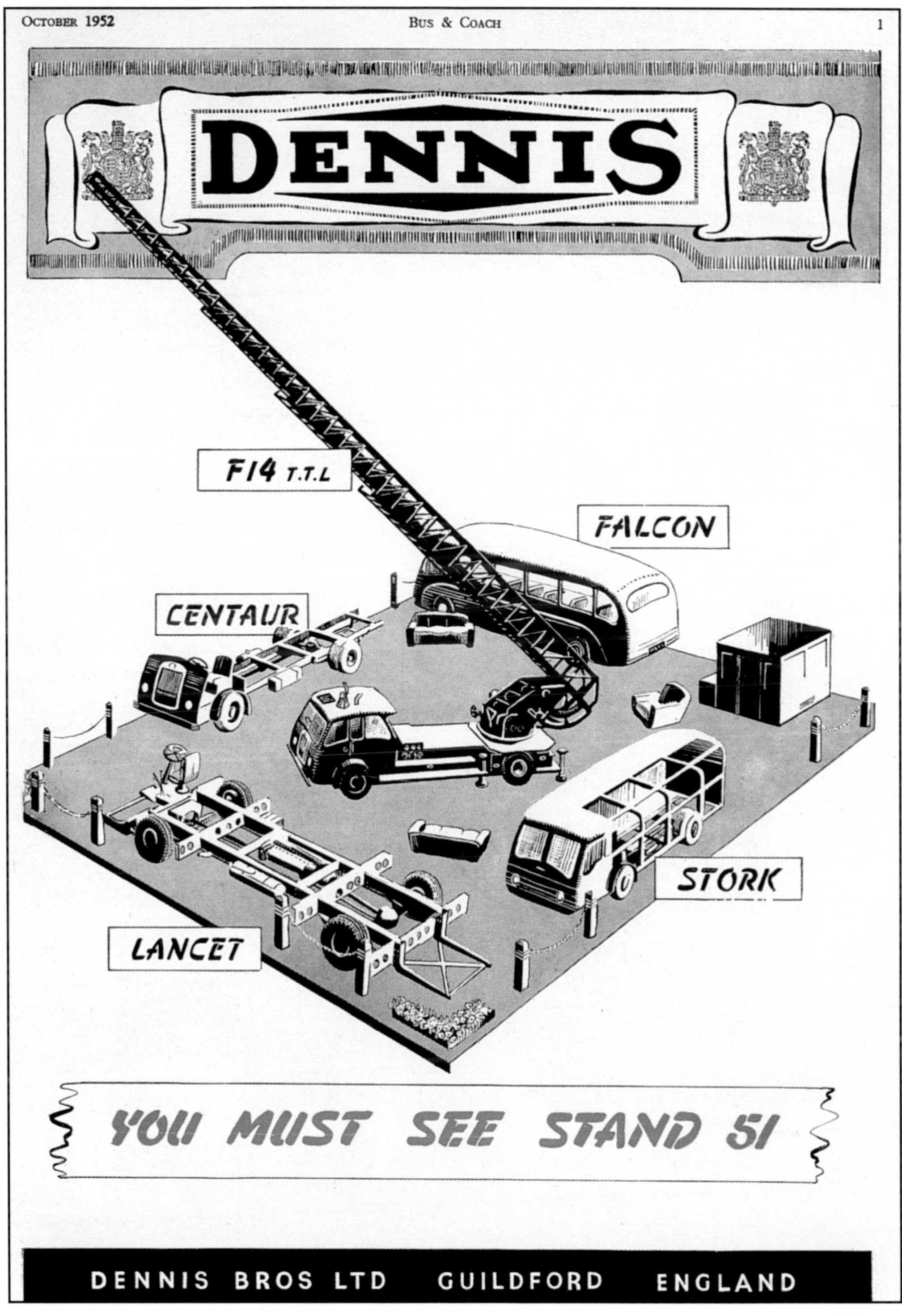

Right:
An advertisement for the 1952 Commercial Motor Show in London showed the products on display, with an F14 fire appliance taking centre stage.

EAST KENT

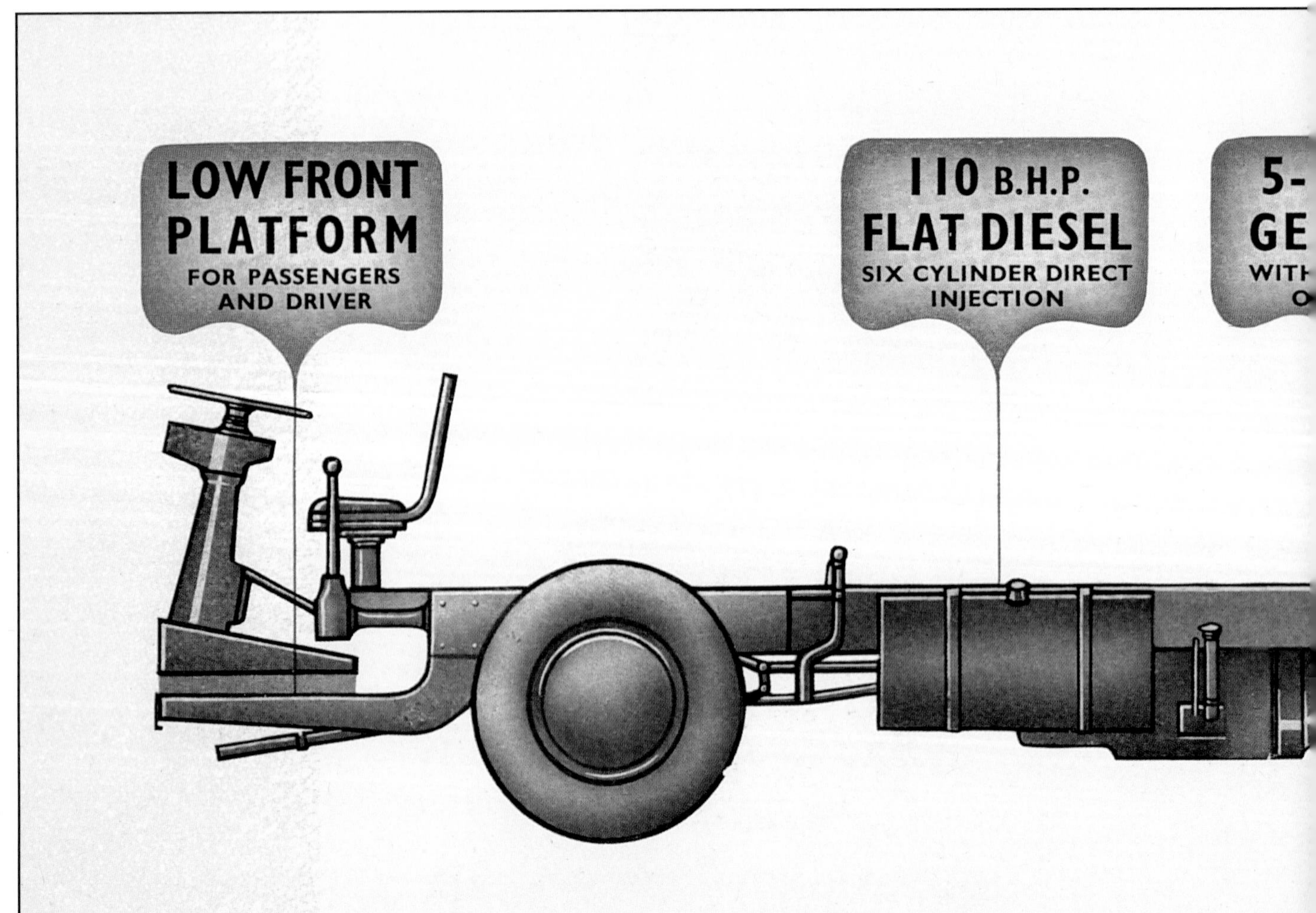
LOW FRONT
PLATFORM
FOR PASSENGERS
AND DRIVER
110 B.H.P.
FLAT DIESEL
SIX CYLINDER DIRECT
INJECTION

Left:
The underfloor-engined Lancet was used for front-line touring duties by the East Kent Road Car Company.

Below:
The Lancet UF's key features portrayed in a 1952 brochure.

municipal vehicles and 57 fire engines. In addition the factory produced 452 lawn mowers.

One of the last major engine developments at Dennis was the introduction in 1953 of a 5.5-litre six-cylinder 87bhp unit. This was installed in the new Centaur 12-ton truck which was designed to plug the gap between the lightweight Pax and the heavy-duty Jubilant. It featured a timber-framed cab of standard Dennis style, had a five-speed gearbox and a two-speed rear axle. From 1954 it was offered with the option of an all-steel cab, and as a tractor unit. Just over 400 Centaurs were built. Production ceased in 1956.

Along with Lancet III coaches, the other area in which Dennis got off to a good start after the war was the supply of fire engines. A new F-series model range was introduced from 1945, starting with the F1. The early F-series were offered with different body styles — the New World and the Braidwood — and were powered either by the 70bhp 3.8-litre Dennis engine or by a 150bhp Rolls Royce B80 straight-eight petrol engine. At this time brigades still used petrol engines, not least because they offered better performance —

> Every operator of passenger carrying vehicles is, if for no other reason, by virtue of his long association with vehicles of one kind or another, the keenest judge of a practical design. Moreover, he has a marked tendency for expressing himself in no uncertain terminology, when occasion demands! And a good thing too, for it is on the basis of the operator's skill in judging the niceties of design — the fine points of superior difference plus the extensive research of Dennis Engineers that the Lancet III has been built.
> — *Lancet brochure, 1950*

and the Rolls Royce engine offered significantly more power than Dennis's own. The F2 could get from 0 to 60mph in a respectable 45 seconds and had a governed top speed of 67mph. In 1946 these figures

SHELL-MEX AND BP LTD
SHELL

E 315
LONDON FIRE BRIGADE
L.C.C
24
DENNIS
SLW 178

Top left:
A new cab for the Centaur, as illustrated in a 1954 brochure showing a Shell-BP tanker.

Left:
A 1956 F101 for London Fire Brigade.
Roger Pennington.

Above:
Open-bodied fire engines were being built for export markets in the 1950s and 1960s. This one is seen in Hong Kong.

would have put any family car to shame.

The fire engine range went through some rapid development. The F1 and F2 both enjoyed long production lives, to 1959 and 1963 respectively. For a period the F1 was also known as the Onslow. The F series comprised a wide range of bespoke models. Best-seller was the F12 with 336 built between 1950 and 1959. The F8, a small limousine appliance for country areas, was another successful model with a reasonably long production life, 245 units between 1952 and 1960. It was built to a width of 6ft 6in, instead of the standard 7ft 6in.

On the bus and coach front the Lancet III was selling fairly well, and was modified to meet new UK Construction & Use regulations, allowing two-axle single-deck buses to be 30ft long and 8ft wide. New axles and a longer wheelbase addressed this need, and increased the seating capacity from 35 to 39 on a typical coach of the day.

But the days of front-engined coaches were numbered. In the quest for ever-greater

> The Dennis Jubilant chassis, produced expressly for the furtherance of economic transport, is enormously strong, amply powered, refined in detail and generous as to equipment.
>
> We make no claim for low initial cost. The outlay is justified by the prospect of the highest order of service, comprising long life, rugged resistance to arduous conditions, easy maintenance, favourable running costs, and a dependability destined to enhance even our own reputation for that quality.
>
> *—Jubilant brochure, c1946*

Above:
The Paravan had a cut away nearside corner with a lift-up door.

passenger capacity, operators and manufacturers were looking at the use of horizontal engines mounted in mid-wheelbase. Dennis developed a horizontal version of the O.6 engine and installed it in a totally new chassis to produce the Dominant. It had an Eaton two-speed axle and a four-speed Hobbs automatic gearbox. As with all early designs of mid-engined bus chassis it was heavy.

So, for 1952 a simpler and lighter model appeared, the Lancet UF. This had a 110bhp version of the horizontal O.6 engine, a single-speed axle and a Dennis five-speed overdrive gearbox. It shaved half a ton off the chassis weight of the Dominant. To give coach passengers the best possible forward view, the driving area was set low in the frame. This was a novel idea in 1952, and 30 years would pass before it came into widespread use. The biggest user of the type was East Kent, with 30 coaches. In Wales, Newport Corporation purchased 11 for use as buses. The last Lancet UFs were built in 1961.

Dennis made one more attempt to cut weight on its mid-engined chassis in the 1950s with the Pelican. It used a horizontal version of the 75bhp 5-litre diesel engine which had powered the Falcon from 1950, uprated to 92bhp and driving through a Meadows gearbox. The chassis weighed a little over 3 tons, and the complete bus was under 6 tons, which was no mean achievement. But when the Pelican appeared in 1956 the boom in the bus and coach market was over. Low prices from high-volume makers such as AEC and Leyland, who between them had captured most of the fleet business, had squeezed Dennis and a number of other smaller manufacturers out. And for operators who required a lighter-duty coach, a 30ft-long model from Bedford had cornered that market.

The slow sales performance of the Lance in what had been a buoyant market convinced the management at Dennis that to succeed in selling double-deck buses it had to provide something which offered a distinct advantage over other products. There was nothing wrong with the Lance — but it was simply no better or no worse than a whole range of similar chassis being produced by other builders.

The company found the answer in a remarkable new chassis which had been developed by Bristol Commercial Vehicles: the Lodekka. This featured a drop-centre rear axle and had the drive offset from the centre line of the chassis, which allowed the gangway in the lower saloon to be dropped by about 12in compared with conventional chassis such as the Lance. This in turn meant that the overall height of the bus was reduced from around 14ft 6in to 13ft 6in — an important consideration in many parts of Britain in the days when an extensive railway network meant a lot of low bridges.

Bristol, which had been nationalised by the Labour government in 1948, could only sell its products to other nationalised companies. Dennis concluded an agreement with Bristol whereby Dennis would manufacture the chassis under licence at Guildford for sale on the open market. Thus was born the Dennis Loline.

It was launched at the 1956 Commercial Motor Show in London with the Gardner 6LW engine as standard. Like the Lance, the Loline came with a choice of four- or five-speed manual gearboxes. Aldershot & District was the first buyer. An improved Loline II came in 1958 with rear air suspension, which was quite a significant advance, even if it didn't really catch on. The frame was revised to allow the fitment of forward-entrance bodywork. The Loline's appeal was broadened by offering AEC and Leyland engines to buyers who did not want the Gardner. Gardner's bigger and more powerful 6LX was also made available.

One Loline II earns a place in history by being the lowest double-deck bus built for operation in Britain. Barton Transport, a large Nottinghamshire operator, had a Loline II chassis fitted with a Northern Counties body with a sunken gangway on the offside of the top deck. This reduced the height to a remarkable 12ft 6in. This was 1ft lower than any other double-decker in service in Britain, and even 0.2m below the 4m height which became a benchmark for double-deck coaches in the 1980s.

A new goods chassis, the 12-ton gross Condor, appeared in 1956 and replaced the Centaur. It was offered as both a rigid and a tractor unit, was powered by the 87bhp 5.5-litre Dennis engine, and featured a new-style cab. Gardner 4LW and 5LW engines were later offered too. Production ended in 1962.

The mainstream heavy lorry market

Below:
The AV series ambulance chassis shows the set-back engine.

Above:
An AV- series ambulance for Sheffield.

became more and more competitive as the 1950s passed. Makes such as AEC, Foden and Leyland were winning most of the heavy business. Bedford, and to a lesser extent Ford and Commer, were doing well in light goods vehicles. Dennis was increasingly becoming a specialist builder, reliant on fire and municipal vehicle sales.

But this realisation, far from curbing the company's aspirations, fuelled a number of imaginative projects as ways were sought to find new niche markets which could be profitably exploited. Innovative products were developed — but in every case volume sales were held back because of high costs. The products might have been what the market wanted — but it was not always willing to pay for them.

The experience gained in building mid-engined bus chassis was applied to goods vehicles in the Stork, which had a horizontal four-cylinder Perkins engine and a set back front axle. This gave good cab access, with a wide door and a low floor. The Stork was a 3-tonner. A Mark 2 Stork had the option of a Perkins six-cylinder engine, and was also marketed in Switzerland as a coach chassis, the SP6.

Another bird of the 1950s was the Heron. This too was a Perkins P4-powered 3-tonner, but with a conventional vertical front-mounted engine. The cab was, however, set forward. It had a new-look cab built at Guildford with crisper styling and a neater grille. This was similar to that fitted from 1956 to the Pax III and to the new 14-ton Hefty which replaced the Max.

The new cab style appeared on fire appliances too, starting with the F24 in 1956, which was fitted with a Rolls Royce B60 six-cylinder engine, coupled to a Rolls Royce four-speed automatic gearbox. At the same time,

> The Condor 12 ton chassis allows more payload and greater body space than is common.
>
> These important considerations are made possible by virtue of the low chassis weight and compact power unit. Carrying the aim of diesel economy to its logical conclusion in providing a vehicle of crisp performance and impressive 'lower end' pulling power, the Condor displays a thriftiness in fuel consumption which varies little with road conditions. With approaching 90 b.h.p. available maximum power is adequate for maintaining tight schedules.
>
> — *Condor brochure, 1956*

On the evening of June 3rd this year a Lancet IV of the State Railways pulled into the Township of Hopetown. It was dusty and mud spattered, but to the people of Hopetown the Lancet was a proud herald of the beginning of a new bus service, believed to be the longest inter-state route in Australia.

Covering 370 miles each way, the Lancet is scheduled for a 15 hours run in each direction, making necessary stops for toilet and refreshment, and the picking up of both passengers and freight.

At present the service is confined to two journeys a week, from Perth on Mondays and Thursdays, returning on Tuesdays and Fridays.

A Passenger Freighter is how the Australians describe the Lancet by virtue of the accommodation provided for 20 passengers and 3 tons of freight, newspapers being among the commodities carried regularly.

Although good roads are experienced, when full use can be made of the overdrive, there are a few sections which are indescribably bad and their negotiation requires skilled driving and robust chassis construction.

— *from* Sidelights, *the Dennis house magazine, summer 1950*

Dennis became the first company to use a Rolls Royce diesel engine in an automotive application, fitting a six-cylinder unit to fire-fighting vehicles for the London and Liverpool fire brigades — the F101 and F102 respectively.

The bonnetted Pax came in for a minor restyle and some new engine options in 1957. It received a wider cab with a single-piece windscreen and the headlights faired into the front wings — small changes, but effective in modernising the truck's appearance. Under the new-look bonnet was the choice of side valve Dennis petrol power or three diesels — the P6 Perkins, Gardner's miserly 4LK or the AEC AV322. The last-named was an unusual four-cylinder version of the more common AV470 six-cylinder as used in fire appliances and a few Loline buses.

The company tried to capitalise on its position as Britain's biggest supplier of fire appliances by developing another emergency service vehicle — the AV-series ambulance. Before World War I ambulance bodies had been built on Dennis chassis, and this continued in the inter-war years. But after the war ambulance authorities had increasingly gone either for coachbuilt bodywork on big car chassis, or high-volume light commercials.

The biggest problem with ambulances, as

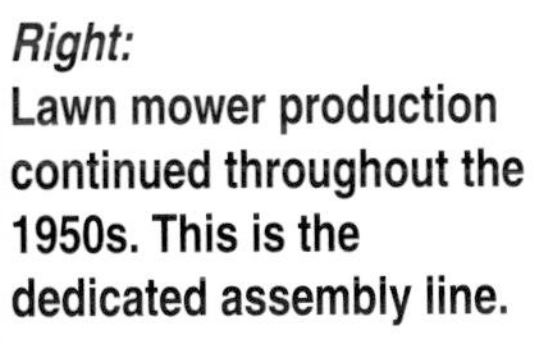

Right:
Lawn mower production continued throughout the 1950s. This is the dedicated assembly line.

Top:
The new Heron, on a 1956 brochure.

Left:
A Heron for Bentalls of Kingston.

any ambulanceman (or woman) will quickly point out, is floor height. On the AV, Dennis got this down to just over 21 inches, which it claimed was lower than any other ambulance. This was achieved by locating the differential to a chassis frame member, with open half-shafts connected to oscillating rear wheels. The front axle was set back — allowing easy entry to the cab — and the engine was located above the axle alongside the driver. For those seeking economy (and not too worried about noise), a 58bhp Perkins P4 diesel was fitted. For performance, the AV could be specified with an Austin Sheerline six cylinder petrol engine. The diesel version was briefly offered as the AG light van.

The AV found buyers in Britain and abroad — over 300 of them — and continued in production until the early 1960s, receiving a re-styled front with a curved windscreen to give it a family resemblance to the company's truck range.

Another specialised vehicle appeared in 1958 — the Paravan. The concept was brilliant. The chassis was a conventional ladder frame with a Perkins P4 diesel located above the front axle. The driver sat ahead of this and the front nearside corner was cut away to leave a wide entrance giving easy access from the kerb to the driving seat ahead of the engine, or to the load area which could be reached to the right as you boarded. The entrance door was a roller shutter which was lifted into the body.

The Paravan was only 6ft 9in wide, had a tight turning circle and was designed for urban

Right and below:
The underfloor-engined Stork lent itself to special bodywork such as the mobile coal office (which had a mock-up fireplace inside) and a Vespa delivery van complete with display area above the driver's cab.

deliveries. Because of the unusually-shaped front, it only had a single centrally-located headlight. It deserved to do well, attacking the problem of urban deliveries from a new angle. But once again it was in a market where price was generally more important than specification. Few were sold — only around 100 — as urban deliveries stayed in the hands of cheaper BMCs and Bedfords.

Fresh ideas kept flowing. Undaunted by the Paravan's poor sales, another even more radical delivery vehicle was built in 1960. The Vendor used front wheel drive, which really was radical at that time. Although the concept wasn't new — it had featured on Citroen cars since the mid-1930s — its use was limited. The trend-setting BMC Mini with front wheel drive had only just appeared, so the Vendor was a bold move.

The use of front wheel drive and independent suspension brought the floor height right down, to under 20 inches. Power was to be supplied by a choice of Standard engines as used in Vanguard cars — a 2.2-litre petrol or a 2.7-litre diesel. But the Vendor was expensive to build and would have been priced accordingly. The complexity of front wheel drive might have frightened potential buyers too, whatever the benefits of a low floor. Dennis envisaged the Vendor being used as a small bus as well as a van — but it did not get beyond the prototype stage.

We have it on good authority that the original performance by a unit called the Dennis Male Voice Choir was in the Borough Hall in 1916, but the present Choir was formed as a section of the Dennis Athletic Club in 1933. Since then it has steadily built up and maintained a very high musical reputation among a wide circle of friends throughout Surrey and the neighbouring counties.

New members are always welcome and the particular need at the moment is for good tenor voices.

L. G. Higgs, Hon. Sec., Dennis Male Voice Choir
— from Sidelights, *the Dennis house magazine, summer 1951*

The 1960s

Struggling to survive

> Maxim — Britain's most dependable 16 ton g.v.w. motorway truck.
> The result of over 70 years specialised experience — maximum power, payload, safety & comfort.
> The 16 ton Dennis Maxim is typical of the range designed to meet the demands of operators requiring 'heavies' having maximum payload capacity and the ability to work motorway schedules with unfailing reliability. Custom-built bodies and traditional Dennis craftsmanship ensure lowest-cost operation and maximum driver comfort on long hauls.
> — *Maxim advert, 1966*

The 1960s started with Dennis producing a mixed range of goods and passenger vehicles. The Lancet underfloor-engined coach was nearing the end of its life. The last was built in 1961, and when Lancet production ended, so did output of the Dennis O.6 engine. The Loline double-decker was selling moderately well, albeit to a limited number of users including the company's staunchest supporter, Aldershot & District.

Further revisions to the Loline frame — mirroring developments in the Bristol Lodekka from which it was derived — allowed a better floor layout in the lower deck of the Loline III model which was introduced in 1961 and continued in production till 1967. A few Loline IIIs had semi-automatic SCG gearboxes.

The Pax goods range was being built in a bewildering variety of specifications, with different combinations of engine, gearbox and wheelbase, and with local authorities still far and away the biggest customers.

Motor mowers were still being built too

Below:
A 1961 F24 for Surrey Fire Brigade.

Top right:
The Delta was essentially a fire appliance. This short-wheelbase model was built as a fuel tanker for Shell-BP.

Above:
A fire engine seen on a tilt-test — a measure of the vehicle's stability. This one is at 35 degrees.

with production averaging 350 a year. Indeed in 1962 the Premier model collected a gold medal at the Southport Flower Show and at the following year's event the Swift rotary grass cutter was described as 'the best introduction of the year'. However the Swift was not in fact a Dennis-built machine; it was produced by a Sussex company and marketed by Dennis.

Fire appliance sales were holding up well. In fact fire sales were becoming increasingly important, and in many places the name Dennis had long been synonymous with fire engines. Dennis claimed to have appliances running in 46 countries.

While high-performance petrol engines remained popular with brigades, a growing number were turning to more economical diesel power. Thus at the start of the 1960s Dennis was offering a wide range of power units to fire chiefs. The Rolls Royce 5.7-litre straight-eight continued with power ratings of 169bhp or a mighty 195bhp. Brigades seeking less power could opt for a 114bhp Jaguar 4.2-litre petrol engine. A six-cylinder Rolls Royce unit was also available. For diesel buyers there was AEC's 125bhp AV470 engine or a 170bhp 12.2-litre Rolls Royce unit. Diesel-powered appliances were allocated model numbers from F101 upwards.

The continued superiority in performance of the high-powered petrol-engined appliances was not in question. For an F110 with AEC engine and Dennis five-speed close-ratio gearbox the company quoted 17 seconds to accelerate from stationary to 30mph. By contrast the Rolls Royce-powered F33 with automatic gearbox could achieve the same speed in just 10 seconds.

Most types were offered in two widths, 7ft and 7ft 6in, and were designed to run at a gross weight of 7tons 15cwt. Front disc brakes became an option from 1962, again demonstrating the company's commitment to technically-advanced solutions to engineering problems. Disc brakes offered greater efficiency and reduced the risk of brake fade

Above:
Open fire appliances were quite a rarity by the 1960s. Johannesburg was among the last buyers to specify an open cab.

on vehicles which by the very nature of their work had to be driven hard.

A significant new fire model was the 1963 Delta. This had the driving position set ahead of the front axle, which allowed the cab to be built substantially lower to accommodate a Simon Snorkel hydraulically-lifted arm. The purposeful-looking Delta was offered with the choice of Rolls Royce petrol or Perkins 6.354 diesel engines.

At the other extreme, where cost was paramount, Dennis was offering a choice of fire appliance bodywork on other makes of chassis such as the Bedford TK.

The tradition of red for fire engines was challenged — briefly — with the delivery to the City of Coventry Fire Brigade of an all-yellow appliance. Yellow was tried as being more visible, which it was in daylight — but under sodium street lights it looked white at night. So red reigned supreme.

Rationalisation of the Pax range was urgently needed and a new Pax IV with a new composite cab was launched at the 1960 Commercial Motor Show in London. The wood-framed cab was built on a steel subframe and used aluminium and glass fibre for the exterior panelling. The previous generation of Pax models was gradually

> The group accounts of Dennis Brothers for the seven months that terminated on April 30 show a pre-tax profit of £63,642, the company states. From this total has to be deducted approximately £26,000 for the cost of taking stock, leaving a balance of £37,642. The statement points out that a 'very large' amount of work still lies ahead to restore the group to full prosperity.
> — *report in* Commercial Motor, *September 1966*

Above:
The Loline was Dennis's last front-engined double-decker for UK operation. Reading Corporation took delivery of this example in 1964.

Right:
The low-frame Loline III chassis.

phased out, including the normal-control types, the last of which were built in 1965. The Pax IV was only offered in a forward-control layout — as were all subsequent Dennis commercials. Both rigids and tractive units were produced with either Perkins 6.305 or BMC 5.1-litre diesels to power them. A few were built to special order with AEC AV322s.

Production of the Jubilant ceased in 1960, but was briefly revived in 1962 with the availability of an eight-wheeler, a rarity indeed in Dennis's output. It was billed with the choice of Gardner 6LW or Dennis 8-litre engines and had an adaptation of the traditional curved-profile cab which had looked quite something 15 years earlier but was a shade old-fashioned in 1962 with its small windscreens.

However it wasn't styling which killed the eight-wheel Jubilant, but legislation. British operators were increasingly turning to articulated lorries to take advantage of changes in the rules on weights and the eight-wheeler, which for over two decades had been the typical British heavy-haulage machine, was about to disappear. The Jubilant's revival was mistimed. Only two were built.

With a huge factory and a declining number of customers, Dennis was heading for difficult times in the early 1960s. In 1962 it bought the fire appliance section of Alfred Miles, followed in 1964 by Mercury, the Gloucester-based manufacturer of specialist tugs for industrial and airport use. Mercury production was transferred to Guildford in 1965.

The truck range was going through yet more change as Dennis struggled to find a niche market. A new Pax V was introduced in the spring of 1963 and ultimately catered for gross weights up to 15 tons. The flexibly-mounted cab inherited from the Pax IV had a high standard of interior trim as the

> One of the most important developments in ambulance design in recent years was the introduction at the last Commercial Motor Show by Dennis Brothers Ltd of its FD4 front-wheel-drive model. The Dennis is possibly unique in being the first ambulance to be designed as such right from the beginning — it has been usual to base ambulances on car, p.s.v. or goods chassis — and it is certainly the first to be built aimed at requirements set out in the report by the Working Party on ambulance training and equipment which was published about 18 months ago.
> — Commercial Motor, *13 June 1969*

four-wheel rigid and seven on the six-wheel rigid. Four different makers' engines were offered, to appeal to as broad a range of potential buyers as possible — AEC AV470, Gardner 5LW, Perkins 6.354, and BMC 5.7-litre. There were three Dennis five-speed gearboxes available — the U, the overdrive UO, and the close-ration UH. The rear axle was either a Dennis spiral bevel or a two-speed Eaton.

Dennis gearboxes, incidentally, were offered with two

Left:
Aldershot & District remained a dedicated Dennis user. This Loline III was among its last. It entered service in 1965.
Peter Durham.

Above:
A Pax IIA goods chassis was modified for use as a bus and bodied by Dennis to evaluate the market for a low-cost rural bus. It remained unique.

Right:
For breweries Dennis offered a six-wheel Pax with a low frame. This one was operated by Flowers.
Peter Davies.

company tried to win business from long-distance hauliers.

There were both artic and rigid Pax Vs, and even though this was supposedly a rationalised range Dennis offered two wheelbases on the tractive unit; five on the power take offs which could be used simultaneously, important for fire appliances where pumps and a compressor or generator were in use.

For brewery fleets, who were significant Dennis customers, low-height models were available with 17in instead of 20in wheels, an option carried over from previous generations of Pax. Over 300 low-loading Pax V rigids were operated by Whitbread, who also ran Pax IV tractor units.

For lighter duties the Heron was still offered, while the Paravan was soldiering on, but now with a conventional front nearside corner.

With an eye on the market for light-duty country buses which had been catered for by the Falcon, Dennis built a neat little bus on a modified Pax IIa chassis in 1965. This had a set back front axle to provide an entrance opposite the driver, and a 32-seat body built by Dennis. It sold for £3,500 complete — but only one was built for UK operation, although some chassis were exported. Later in the decade a pair of Pax truck chassis would be bodied as buses for operation in Llandudno. These were to be the last bus bodies built in Guildford.

The body shop, as well as building cabs and fire appliances, produced ambulance bodies for fitment to other makes of chassis including Bedford and Karrier. It was also busy making refuse collectors, with the Paxit compactor-type growing in popularity to the point where the Tippax was dropped from the range in 1965.

The company had its eye on the top end of the truck weight range, and in 1964 announced the Maxim tractor unit, suitable for operation at up to 26/28 tons gross, and later raised to 30 tons, then the legal maximum on Britain's roads. A rigid 16-ton four-wheeler was also available, and a 22-ton six-wheeler. This was a well-specified truck with power steering, automatic chassis lubrication and — wait for it — a heater as standard. However it lacked a tilt cab, and Dennis's claim that the cab could

Above:
The Maxim tractor unit offered low weight and high payload capacity. It was originally powered by a Cummins engine, but later models used Perkins power.

> The idea that only a giant can do the job is no longer valid. Try Dennis.
> — *truck leaflet, 1970*

Right:
The acquisition of Mercury saw the factory at Guildford producing tugs such as this for British Rail.

Right:
Mercury's top-power aircraft tugs were fitted with scaled-down Dennis scuttles.

Overleaf:
A D-series water tender for Suffolk Fire Service. New in 1969 it had a Rolls Royce engine.
Roger Pennington.

be removed in just 15 minutes seemed like an inadequate response to that criticism.

A new source of power was selected for the Maxim, available in both rigid and artic guises. This was the 7.7-litre V8 Cummins, built in Darlington, and rated at 185bhp. That was to prove a serious mistake. The Cummins engine turned out to be unreliable, as manufacturers other than Dennis also learned to their cost, and from 1965 the Maxim was offered with the V8.510 Perkins which was a rather better bet but, with only 170bhp on tap, left the Maxim underpowered for top-weight operation.

Despite a low unladen weight which maximised its load-carrying capabilities, the Maxim was another model which enjoyed but limited sales success.

For lighter artics, the Pax 22 — to run at 22 tons gross — was announced in 1966 with

SUFFOLK FIRE SERVICE
FELIXSTOWE
PETROL

YRT 974H

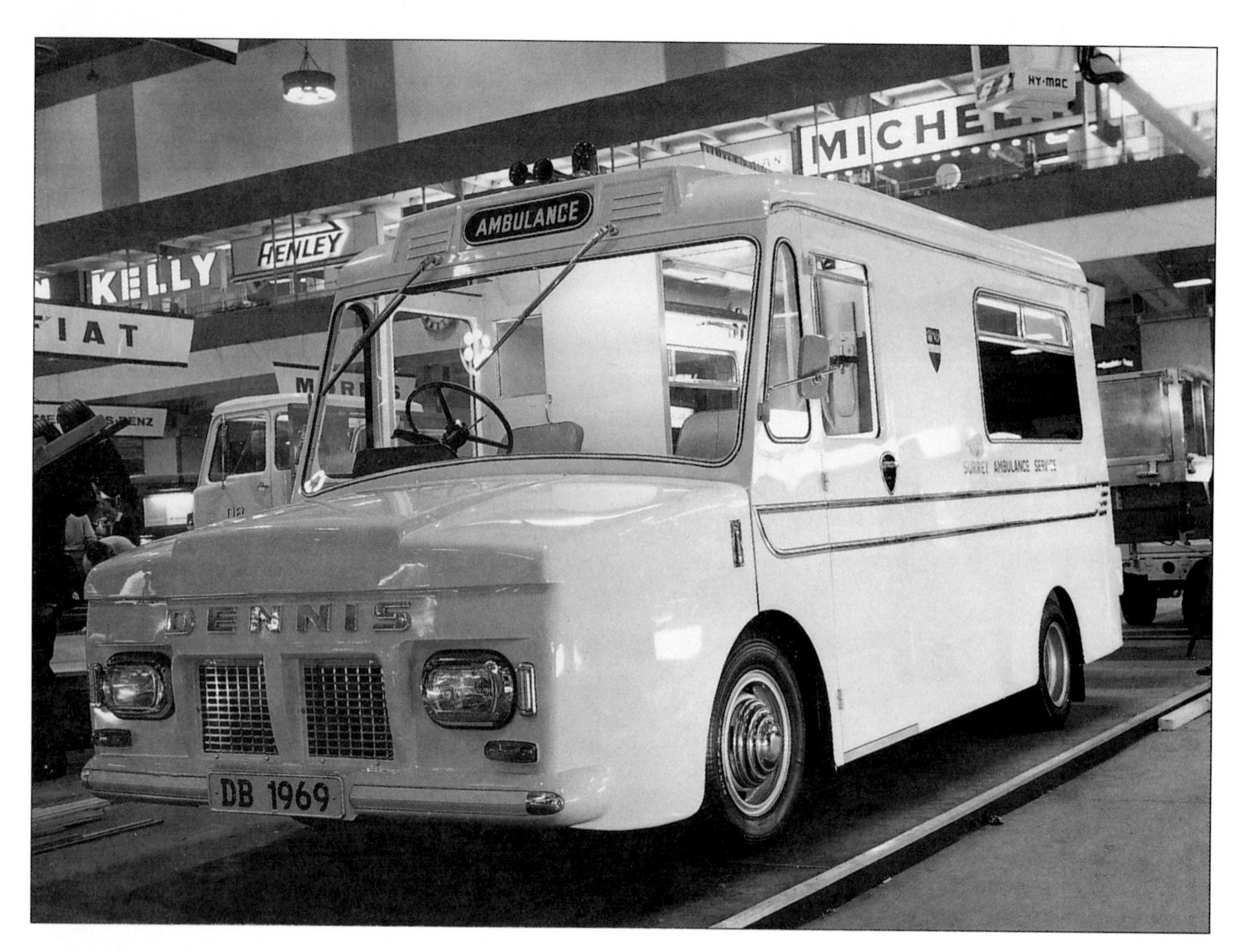

Above:
The technically-advanced front-wheel-drive ambulance.

a Perkins 6.354 engine. It had a short life and during 1968 the Pax range finally was really rationalised, with just two models, a new 15-ton four-wheeler and a six-wheel brewery low-loading model which only lasted until 1969. New Paxit (40cu yd) and Paxit Major (50cu yd) refuse bodies were produced for the 15-tonner.

The Pax V cab and modified Pax chassis formed the basis of one Mercury model, the MD120, powered by a Perkins 6.354 engine driving through a torque convertor transmission and with a drawbar pull of 120,000lbs. The Mercury range spanned models from the MD40 (4,000lbs drawbar pull), designed for use in railway stations up to the massive MD400 aircraft tug which was powered by an AEC V8 engine. Only two MD400s were built.

An uprated front axle in 1970 took the gross weight of the Pax to 15½ tons and at the same time the name was dropped, the new model being the DB 15.5. There was also a DB 15 tipper. The letters indicated Dennis Brothers and the new models were — sometimes — badged as Dominants. A tractive unit was soon added, the DB 24T Defiant, with a turbocharged Perkins engine. The DB range used a glass fibre cab, built in Guildford.

The company lost money in 1965 — £90,000 — and management consultants were brought in. The 1966 annual general meeting had to be postponed as a group of shareholders called for changes in the board. Changes were made, and the company returned to profit in 1966 — but it wasn't out of the woods.

By 1967 the tide was turning firmly against front-engined double-deck buses. Dennis had sold 280 Lolines over 10 years, with just over half going to Aldershot & District. Now it took stock of its position. Some urban operators were switching to one-person-operated single-deckers; others to rear-engined double-deckers. To compete in either of these markets would require considerable investment to develop totally new models, with no guarantee of a return. Dennis decided the time was ripe to bow out, and to concentrate its resources on lorries and fire appliances. Although Dennis had been building buses since its early days, it was only in the 1970s that the seeds were sown which would lead to the company building more buses than ever before. But that was not something which anyone could have anticipated as the last Loline left the factory gates in 1967.

By the end of the 1960s all was not well. The company had pulled out of selling buses. It had introduced new and uprated trucks, but failed to make any significant impact on the

'Burning time' is the principal enemy of Fire Brigades and anything which the vehicle manufacturer can do to reduce it gives the fireman a better chance of controlling the blaze. The excellent acceleration and manoeuvrability of the compact 'D' series reduces the journey time, and the fast priming speed of the Dennis No.2 pump coupled with a general ease of handling of the controls, enables water to be brought into play with the minimum of delay.

Even after considering the high stresses suffered from the hard driving of this emergency vehicle, the high engineeering standards and conscientious inspection procedures enable Dennis Brothers to offer a 2 year guarantee with the 'D' series fire fighting vehicle.

— D series brochure, 1969

haulage market, which is where the high sales potential was.

It decided to concentrate on the areas where it was strongest — the production of municipal vehicles and fire appliances, both low volume bespoke products with a high labour content. But this meant that the company simply wasn't getting the throughput it needed to remain viable. Change was in the air.

One specialist truck builder who was selling well to hauliers did take a look at Dennis with a view to buying it. Seddon of Oldham was the company — but in the end it decided not to proceed.

Instead the company was bought by the Hestair group — after a vigorous defence by the Dennis board which was opposed to the take over. The deal was signed in early 1972. The company was valued at £3.4 million.

Below:
Goods vehicle sales were dwindling. A local removal company bought this Pax V pantechnicon.

Rationalisation

Do what you do do well

Hestair had been formed in 1970 with the take-over of the former Heston Airport company by David Hargreaves, backed by Bankers Trust International. The first vehicle company it acquired was Yorkshire Vehicles, makers of tankers and road sweeper bodies. This,

> High fuel economy engines have been chosen for the Dominator and modest weight plus component strength make for economy and low downtime. The use of an integral retarder extends brake and drum life many times and automatic chassis lubrication cuts service time.
> *— Dominator brochure, 1981*

Left:
The Hestair Dennis line-up in 1979: the first Dominator is in the centre, flanked by a fire appliance and a refuse collection vehicle. On the outside are export vehicles, destined for Libya.

Above:
A mid-1970s Delta skip-loader.

incidentally, was the successor to the Yorkshire Patent Steam Wagon Co, whose main claim to fame was to renounce the internal combustion engine as having no future. (Its competitor on the other side of the Pennines, the Lancashire Steam Motor Co, took the opposite view and later became Leyland Vehicles.)

Then Hestair bought Eagle Engineering, manufacturers of tankers and refuse bodies. Both companies' turnover totalled somewhere in the region of £1.5 million out of a total Hestair group turnover of £4 million. The acquisition of Dennis — turnover £12 million — was a big move for Hestair.

Hestair took over Dennis when production was at an all-time low. It acquired a huge factory, still producing a lot of componentry in-house. It immediately sold the site at Woodbridge, renting back those areas which were needed to maintain production — about two-thirds of the buildings. This provoked accusations of asset stripping, but Hestair argued that with losses approaching £1 million, something had to be done.

There were boardroom changes, and the company's products and business activities were put under the microscope. One of the last developments under the previous management had been a high-performance front wheel drive ambulance, designed to give the low floor so sought after by ambulance crews. This had a 140bhp 2.8-litre Jaguar engine, a Borg Warner automatic gearbox and independent suspension. It was a far cry from the standard ambulance of the day, offering handling and ease of access which 25 years later has still to be matched.

But it suffered from the perennial problem of cost. That it was good there was no doubt — but it was just too expensive. Sadly, the project was canned.

The manufacture of Dennis-Mercury tugs was axed and that part of the business sold to Marshalls of Halifax. Lawnmower production went to Hestair's farm equipment division in Kent. Axle production, too, was brought to an end. The total income from Hestair's rationalisation, including the sale of the site, was roughly equivalent to the price which it had paid for the company.

This left Hestair Dennis, as the company now traded, with its core business of fire appliances and trucks aimed at local authorities. The fire appliances were now using two engines, the Rolls Royce B81 petrol and the Perkins V8.510 diesel. The small D-series model, only 7ft wide, joined the established F-series range and had a 4.2-litre Jaguar petrol

Above:
The Alleycat was a narrow-width refuse-collection vehicle, which was designed to penetrate city areas.

engine. This engine was not a success and was soon replaced by the Rolls Royce B61.

There was also a brief involvement in aircraft crash tenders at this time, with Dennis building bodywork on almost 100 Thornycroft Nubian 6x6 chassis for the Ministry of Defence.

The new management looked at Dennis's involvement in the haulage business, where very small numbers of vehicles were still being sold and reached a decision which was long overdue — to pull out. Sales were low, and so were profits. It was a business best left to high-volume builders.

The company's core products were out of date, both fire engines and refuse collection vehicles. Consequently it had a small share of each market — 20 per cent or less — and virtually no export business. Production was down to around 300 vehicles a year which was insufficient to generate any profit. And by the end of 1974 the company was getting uncomfortably close to its £1 million overdraft limit.

This was the time of three-day-week working in much of British industry because of the need to conserve electricity during the prolonged strike by coal miners. However an early investment by Dennis Brothers ensured full-time employment for the workforce at Guildford. The 60-year-old Sulzer-powered generating plant was still intact, and enjoyed unexpected importance, being activated in the periods when the company was not allowed to consume power generated by the state-owned electricity board.

Having pruned uneconomic activities the question was: what next? Oil prices had risen rapidly in 1973 and many countries in the Middle East had suddenly grown rich and were awash with funds. Coincidentally, many had been long-standing buyers of Dennis fire engines and municipal vehicles, with links dating back to the days of the British Protectorate after World War I.

New managing director John Smith looked abroad, and started cultivating markets where there was a demand for a simple robust truck

— and won a growing number of orders. Dennis was soon selling to Iraq, the Gulf States and Libya. The last-named bought many hundreds of Dennis Delta 16-tonners and was central to the company's survival.

In areas where there was little piped water, for example, Firebird and Waterbird fire appliances were built on 16-ton chassis designed to carry the maximum amount of water with the minimum of bodywork. Some 800 municipal vehicles were sold to the Middle East too, including refuse collectors, cesspool emptiers and skip loaders.

Sales climbed — and profits with them. The profits generated from sales to the booming Middle East countries were ploughed back into product development by Hestair so that Dennis could recover its pre-eminent position in the UK fire and municipal markets.

In the UK fire appliance business, ERF were market leaders in the mid-1970s, followed closely by Dodge using a modified truck chassis with a Perkins V8.510 engine. The F-series which was being built by Dennis had an expensive integral cab with an ash frame covered in aluminium. It was a high-quality product, but too expensive to be competitive.

A new rationalised range of fire appliances, the R-series (for Retained fire stations), was introduced in 1976, confirming the company's continued commitment to its oldest market. These were developed with a new separate glass fibre crew cab mounted on an uprated air-braked F-series chassis. The new model was much less expensive to build and its arrival on the market coincided with a decision by ERF to cease production of fire appliances and concentrate on trucks.

The R-series was soon a best-seller and by fitting the Perkins V8.640 (which the Dodge chassis could not accommodate) it contributed to a Dennis market share in excess of 40 per cent by 1978. The new range was offered only with diesel power. It had taken over 20 years, but brigades had finally accepted a new generation of diesel engines whose performance could match that of the Rolls Royce petrol unit which was now an option.

However Dennis recognised that for all its products it needed a modern tilt cab which would meet the influential Swedish cab impact tests. To do this would require a steel rather than a glass fibre structure. Ogle Designs were commissioned to style a new crew cab range suitable for a fire engine (six-man crew) and a municipal vehicle (five man crew with single-door low entry) as well as a standard day cab.

In the interim a Motor Panels steel cab was offered in those territories where glass fibre was considered unsuitable. This cab was the same as that supplied by Motor Panels to Foden and in the late 1970s was fitted to some 500 trucks for the Middle East, mainly two- and three-axle tankers.

The Ogle-designed cab went into production at Guildford in 1979, in a new purpose-built facility. A non-tilting version was fitted to an extensively-modified R-series fire appliance chassis, to create the new RS model, with the first being supplied to Manchester Fire Service. By this time Girling Skidcheck anti-lock brakes were a standard fitment. Production of the RS and the sister SS model continued through to the beginning of 1995, with the last being delivered to Cleveland fire brigade. Over 1,750 were sold, making the RS/SS range the most successful Dennis fire model ever, in terms of sales volumes. A narrow version of the cab was used to create the 7ft wide DS.

The new Ogle cab was also fitted to refuse collection vehicles. A new model was evolved with asymmetric rear springs and a set-back front axle, tailored specifically to the needs of rear-loading refuse collectors where the compaction mechanism imposed a considerable weight on the rear axle. By moving the front axle to a position where it was almost behind the cab, and by getting the rear axle close to the back of the vehicle, thanks to the asymmetric springs, it was possible to load the vehicle to its maximum capacity without overloading the rear axle.

The development of the new chassis and the adoption of the Ogle cab coincided with work being done by sister company Hestair Eagle on a new compaction mechanism. This was adopted by Dennis (replacing a system licensed from Swiss company Ochsner) and the new model was known as the Phoenix. It

> Dennis produced in 1908 its first fire engine and since then Dennis fire engines have been exported to more than 75 countries in every part of the globe. More recently the company moved into the field of municipal vehicles and these too have been tremendously successful with Dennis refuse collection vehicles operating in countries as diverse as Iraq, Hong Kong, Australia, Libya, Holland, Nigeria and Chile, as well as claiming half the United Kingdom market.
> *— brochure, c1982*

was another success. It boosted the market share of Dennis and Eagle to 50 per cent — and led to the demise of Shelvoke & Drewry who just six years before had been market leaders with a 65 per cent share.

As well as revamping the fire and municipal ranges, attention was turned once more to other areas of activity which looked as though they offered scope for growth. One did. The other didn't.

The Dominator re-established Dennis as a major player in the bus market. Key customers included *(left top)* Leicester City Transport, *(left below)* the Scottish Bus Group and (*above*) South Yorkshire Transport.
M. Fowler, Stewart J. Brown, Gavin Booth

The market which did prove worth exploring was that for buses and coaches. Conditions in the British market had changed dramatically in the 10 years since Loline production had ended. The formation of the giant British Leyland empire was reducing the choices available to bus operators as Leyland rationalised its product ranges. There were also complaints about BL being unresponsive to customers' requests for deviations from standard specifications.

The stage was set for some new competition, and Dennis was poised to provide it. Its new generation bus chassis had to meet some key operating criteria in terms of reliability, running costs and ease of repair. Gardner was widely respected as the builder of engines which gave operators both durability and low fuel costs, and it was to Gardner that Dennis turned for power for their first new model — not that there was a lot of choice.

Amidst concern about brake lining life and in anticipation of ever-tightening legislation on braking, the new model had to have an automatic gearbox with a retarder. Here the German gearbox specialists, Voith, were in the lead and work was put in hand to develop the as yet untried combination of Gardner engine and Voith gearbox. A front-mounted radiator was fitted to improve cooling, a recognised problem on early rear-engined buses with the radiator alongside the engine.

In what has to be one of the most unusual tests of the driveline for an all-new bus chassis, a Gardner 6LXB engine and Voith gearbox were fitted to a 15-year-old front-engined Daimler which was tried in service by a number of operators, including London who, little more than a decade later, were to become a major Dennis customer — although not for double-deckers.

The idea behind the re-engineered Daimler was simple: it provided a mobile test bench where the engine and gearbox would be operating in real traffic, being driven by real drivers. It was a much more realistic test than could have been obtained on any 1970s laboratory equipment.

While the mobile test bench was clocking up the miles and proving the compatibility of the chosen engine/gearbox combination, the engineering team at Guildford were developing a steel-suspended chassis which would be available initially in three lengths — a nominal 9.5m and 10.3m for double-deck bodywork and 11m for single-deck operation.

The idea of using the same chassis for both double-deck and single-deck bodywork was as old as the history of the motorbus, but few manufacturers had tried it with rear-engined models. For those who had, success had been mixed — as it was to prove for Dennis.

Development work completed, Dennis

Left:
Thought to be the only bus ever to stop outside the residence of the British Prime Minister at London's 10 Downing Street, the first Dennis Dominator took members of the company's management to collect an export award.

Right:
Managing director John Smith received the award from the then Prime Minister, James Callaghan, and presented the premier with a model of a Delta fire appliance in exchange.

unveiled its new bus model — the Dominator — in 1977. The first was bodied as a double-decker by East Lancashire Coachbuilders of Blackburn, a company which was to figure prominently in the early days of Dominator production.

The new model quickly found buyers. Many urban fleets in Britain tried the Dominator. For some, such as Leicester CityBus and South Yorkshire Transport, it quickly became their standard double-decker. With over 300 in operation by 1986, South Yorkshire became the biggest Dominator operator. Many of South Yorkshire's Dominators had Rolls Royce Eagle engines and air suspension, the latter initially an option but later a standard feature. While the vast majority of Dominators had Voith gearboxes, in response to customer demand a small number were built with the short-lived Maxwell automatic. The most unusual customer was the fire service in Tyne & Wear, which had a long-wheelbase Dominator bodied as a mobile emergency control centre.

Sales success depends on a broad base of customers, and this the Dominator achieved in the first half of the 1980s. It established Dennis as a supplier to the Scottish Bus Group, at that time easily Scotland's largest bus operator, and it also helped open up

Above:
The front-engined Jubilant was developed specifically for Hong Kong. Kowloon Motor Bus took 364.

overseas business in an important market for British bus builders — Hong Kong.

But before the Dominator gained acceptance in Hong Kong, Dennis found a call for a rather different type of bus. Hong Kong's major bus operators had, in the early 1970s, introduced new rear-engined models from British Leyland with varying degrees of success. Kowloon Motor Bus in particular was concerned about falling standards of service reliability and, as an interim measure, decided that it needed a new type of front-engined bus which had an entrance opposite the driver to make it suitable for one person operation. This would provide operational reliability on the streets of Hong Kong while work was put in hand to ensure that future designs of rear-engined models would be able to cope with Hong Kong's arduous operating conditions — high temperatures, high humidity, steep hills and — the bus operator's dream — constant heavy loads throughout the day.

Dennis had for many years been the major supplier of fire appliances to Hong Kong, so had a proven reputation for sound engineering. To meet KMB's demands Dennis produced the Jubilant, which used the now proven Gardner/Voith combination but instead of having it mounted transversely across the rear of the chassis, it was mounted in-line at the front. In all 364 Jubilants were supplied to KMB between 1977 and 1984. Thirty were ordered by Hong Kong's other major operator, China Motor Bus, and one was supplied to City Tramways in Cape Town. Ten years and many millions of miles later in Dennis's centenary year, all 364 of KMB Jubilants remain in daily use, a tribute to the soundness of the concept. It is estimated that around one million people a day travel on Dennis buses in Hong Kong.

Having won business in Hong Kong and then shown it could deliver a reliable vehicle, Dennis set about developing the Dominator to meet Hong Kong's needs for a reliable rear-engined bus. To provide maximum carrying capacity — up to 172 people at peak loading times — the answer was to add a third axle, raising the gross weight from 16 to 22 tons. Thus was born the biggest chassis ever to

Above:
From the outset the Dominator was designed to be suitable for use as a single-decker too. One unusual application for the chassis was as a mobile control unit for the Tyne & Wear fire service.
Gavin Booth

leave Guildford in the shape of the tri-axle Dragon and Condor models, for KMB and China Motor Bus respectively. By 1992 KMB had bought 1,000 buses from Dennis. To cope with the extra weight the engine was uprated from the 180bhp 6LXB used in the UK-specification two-axle Dominator, to the 230bhp 6LXCT. The healthy Hong Kong business helped Dennis survive the sharp down-turn in demand for buses in Britain in the early 1980s.

The market which in the end proved not to be worth pursuing was that for trucks in the UK. Buoyed up by the Delta's success abroad, the decision was made to offer it in the UK from 1978, initially with a 155bhp Perkins T6 power unit and, from 1981, with the option of a 180bhp Gardner 6LXB. The Delta did find a few customers in Britain, the biggest being British Oxygen. It was also used by the London Philarmonic Orchestra and by Thames Television, but sales volumes were never high enough to make it a viable proposition. Dennis ended up building around 20 trucks a year for the UK market — all to odd specifications which the high-volume manufacturers were unwilling to touch. The middle east markets were contracting rapidly too and this finally killed the Delta off in 1983. It was Hestair-Dennis's final involvement with trucking.

The Dominator opened the door for another new Dennis model, the mid-engined single-deck Dorchester, built between 1983 and 1987. This was designed to meet the needs of Scottish Bus Group companies who wanted the advantages of Gardner economy in a coach. Dorchesters were built for Western Scottish and Central Scottish. Some were used on SBG's prestigious Scottish Citylink long-distance coach services. Others performed on medium-distance bus services in central Scotland and for this Dennis produced an 11m model with Voith automatic transmission. Dorchester coaches had ZF manual gearboxes. With the Dorchester it was a case of where Dennis led, others followed:

Top:
More typical of single-deck Dominators is this high-capacity bus in service in Chester.

Right:
The low-cabbed Delta Simon Snorkel fire appliance. This one was operated by Cheshire.

Dennis's success with the Dorchester prompted Leyland to change its engine policy and offer Gardner engines in its Tiger range.

Small numbers of Dorchesters were sold to other coach operators, but here Dennis's main model was the lighter-duty Lancet. The Lancet was launched in 1980 and was aimed at both coach operators and at bus companies looking for a mid-range chassis with lower costs than heavy duty models like the Dorchester and similar chassis from other manufacturers. It was offered with a wide choice of engines — Leyland 402 and 411, Perkins 6.354 and T6.354 and even the

DENNIS

DENNIS
LOW 305R

Left top:
A Delta 6x4 water tanker for Iraq.

Left below:
A 1976 R-series water tender, among the last appliances with the old-style cab. ***Roger Pennington***

Right:
The new-look RS-series fire appliance, with Ogle-designed cab.

Below:
The RS quickly became a best-seller. A 1978 model used by Windsor fire brigade seen outside the town's famous Castle. ***Roger Pennington***

Perkins V8.540. These offered power outputs ranging from 124 to 180bhp.

Where the Dorchester was designed primarily as a maximum-length 12m coach, the Lancet was offered in lengths from 8 to 11m. It introduced Dennis to a number of fleets — and helped pave the way for a significant new model later in the decade. Not all Lancets were coaches. Bus-bodied Lancets were operated by, among others, the Scottish Bus Group, Blackpool Transport, Leicester CityBus, Merseyside Transport and West Midlands Travel who had a pair delivered in 1986 which were fitted with wheelchair lifts — an early example of a British bus operator providing transport for people with mobility handicaps which was another area in which Dennis was later to feature. The Lancet found some export custom — notably in Bermuda — and was also used as the basis of a small number of mobile libraries in Britain. Production ceased in 1988, with the launch of a significant new chassis offering benefits available from neither the Lancet or the Dorchester.

The early 1980s were busy times for the design team at Dennis, with new bus models

appearing with remarkable rapidity. The single-deck Dominator had found but a few customers, but showed that there was a demand for a single-deck chassis. The next development was the appearance in 1980 of the Falcon. This offered a low frame and maximum passenger capacity with its

horizontal Gardner 6HLXB or turbocharged 6HLXCT engine in the rear overhang, driving through either an SCG or a Voith automatic gearbox.

The Falcon was in fact conceived as a family of models — a low-frame bus, a standard-frame coach and the novel Falcon V. The Falcon V was technically the most interesting. For coach operation it was powered by a rear-mounted Perkins TV8.640 (the only automotive use of a turbocharged Perkins 640 engine). It was also offered as a double-deck bus chassis with a Mercedes-Benz V6 unit — the only use of a Mercedes power unit in a Dennis psv chassis. The Mercedes engine was rated at 280bhp, making

Left: top
The final Delta trucks used the Ogle-designed cab.

Left: below
The Ogle cab was also used for an updated range of refuse collection vehicles.

Right:
The Scottish Bus Group was a key Dorchester customer, with a number being used on the high-profile Scottish Citylink express coach network.

Below:
The Dorchester was suitable for either bus or coach bodywork. This Dorchester was the first Dennis to be bodied by Dutch coachbuilder Berkhof.

the Falcon the most powerful product from Guildford when it was announced. Only a small number of Falcon Vs were produced as double-deckers and were developed with a '10 per cent' target — 10 per cent weight reduction, 10 per cent cost saving, and 10 per cent more passengers.

But the Falcon was in essence an urban single-deck chassis, and it performed in this role with a number of operators including companies in the British Bus group. Production came to an end in 1993 when the horizontal Gardner engine being used was overtaken by tight new European legislation on exhaust emissions.

At the other extreme from the sophisticated air-suspended Falcon was the Dart, a rugged front-engined single-deck bus chassis, available with left- or right-hand drive. It had a high frame and steel suspension and was designed for tough export markets. Few were sold and all went to South Africa where they were fitted with the locally-produced Atlantis diesel engine. A rugged underfloor-

Above and right:
The light-duty Lancet not only found buyers in the bus and coach business in Britain and overseas, but was also popular among libraries. A Lancet rural bus is seen *(above)* with Northern Scottish in Aberdeenshire. The mobile library *(right)* was supplied to Staffordshire.

Left:
The Domino midibus in service in Manchester. It was developed specifically for high-frequency city service.

engined model, the Arrow, was also sold in South Africa and fitted with an Atlantis engine. The Durban Transport Management Board was the only taker.

At this time Dennis was also involved in an experiment with an alternative power source — electricity. The last new trolleybus built for use in Britain had entered service in 1962. In 1984

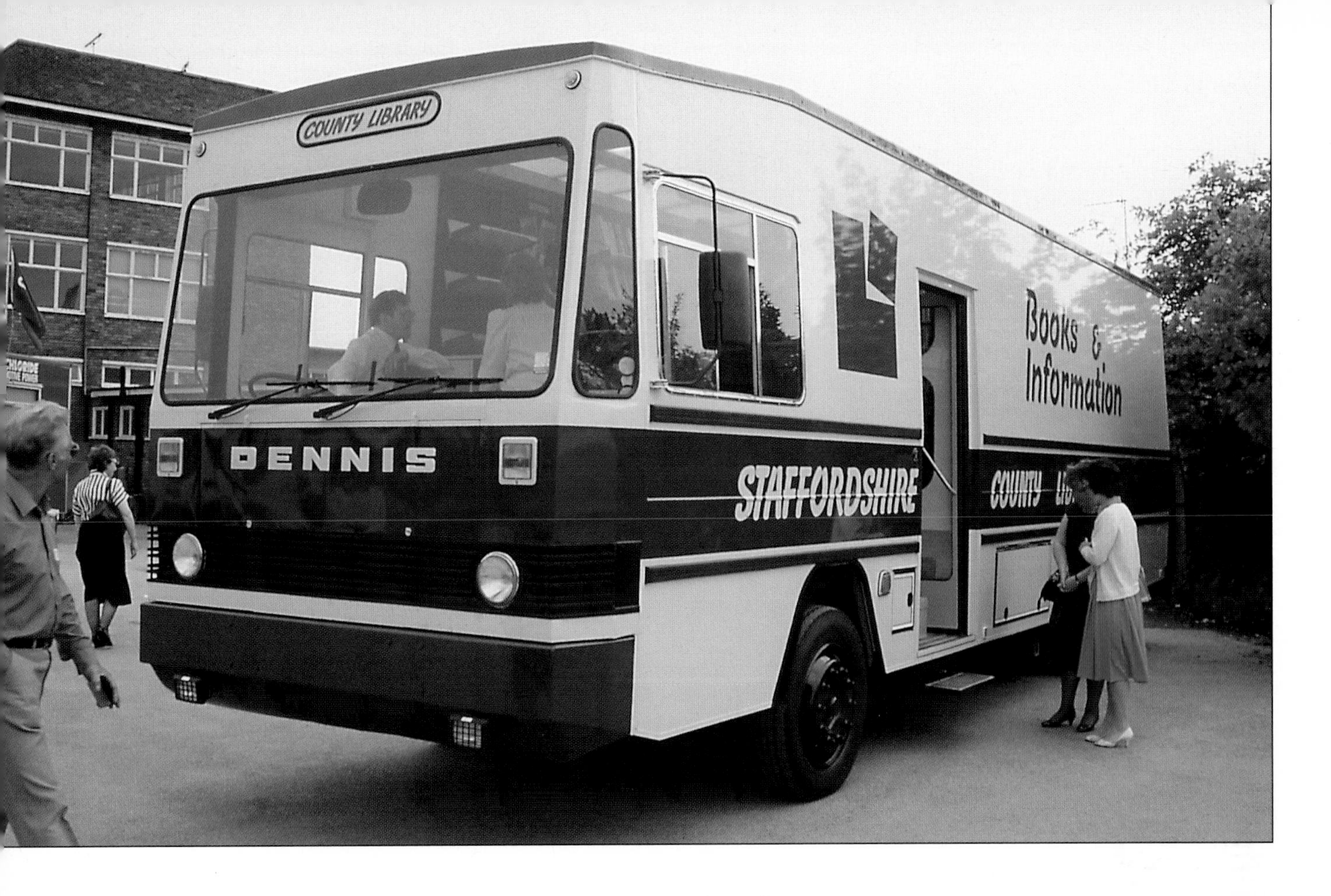

a Dennis Dominator had the distinction of being the first-ever electrically-powered vehicle from Guildford, and Britain's first trolleybus for over 20 years.

The chassis had a GEC traction motor in the rear overhang and a Dorman three-cylinder diesel engine to provide auxiliary power. The bus was built for the South Yorkshire Passenger Transport Executive and was tried out on a test track at Doncaster racecourse. But against a background of reduced government funding for public transport, the Dennis trolleybus remained a trial vehicle and never entered revenue-earning service. It may well prove to be the last trolleybus to be built in Britain.

Steve Burton joined Hestair Dennis from Leyland Vehicles in 1982 as production director, taking over as managing director from Hestair chairman David Hargreaves in 1985. A rationalisation programme soon followed. Dennis was still building bodies for fire engines and for refuse collection vehicles — and the latter activity was also being carried out in Warwick by Hestair Eagle. Both companies had their own competing sales teams.

The decision was made that each part of Hestair's vehicle empire should build those products at which it excelled. Thus Guildford would concentrate on chassis for fire appliances and buses and coaches. Hestair Eagle would build refuse collection vehicles, adopting the Dennis chassis — and creating the successful Dennis Eagle range. At the same time production of cabs was moved from Guildford to Blackpool, where Hestair had recently taken over Duple Coachbuilders and with them the appropriate skills for cab production.

And it was decided to give up fire engine body production which was uneconomic because of the great variety in fire authorities' requirements.

As a result the Dennis factory became focussed on two key markets, fire and psv chassis. This rationalisation allowed Hestair to sell off for development a part of the site which they had actually bought back — and make a profit in the booming property market of the mid-1980s. And it also stemmed the losses being incurred on the Guildford operations.

The rationalisation of the Guildford site came as the major part of Britain's bus industry was being privatised and deregulated. The management at Dennis could see that in a new competitive and cost-conscious operating environment operators would be looking for different types of buses. This was a major opportunity for the company — and it was to prove a major blow to Dennis's competitors whose product ranges were geared to the needs of the old order and some of whom spent too much time trying to ensure a future for their existing models instead of developing

Above:
Britain's last trolleybus was a Dennis. It was built in collaboration with GEC and the South Yorkshire Passenger Transport Executive to explore the feasibility of re-introducing trolleybuses to Britain's streets.

> The Dennis Javelin coach chassis changes the economics of the passenger transport business. The hitherto unobtainable combination of light weight and low initial cost with the high performance and long life durability of the premium heavyweight is now a reality.
>
> Advanced design techniques allied to innovative engineering gives the Javelin significant weight savings — up to 15% less than conventional heavyweight chassis — to the benefit of fuel economy. The light weight is not achieved at the expense of reliability or durability, as the Javelin design uses premium quality componentry throughout.
>
> Cost conscious operators now have a truly versatile coach with the power for long hauls and the economy necessary for profitability on short distance work.
>
> — *Javelin brochure*

new ones.

In response to requests from Greater Manchester Transport, a new midibus was introduced in 1984. This was a heavy-duty vehicle designed for intensive city centre operation and had a rear-mounted Perkins engine driving through a Maxwell gearbox to a rear axle based on that used in the double-deck Dominator. This made it expensive. It was evaluated by London Transport, and an order was received from South Yorkshire Transport. Although only 34 were built, the Domino was a pointer to the future when a simpler and less expensive midibus was to play a key part in Dennis's growing success.

Whatever the considerable merits of the Gardner engine range, a growing number of bus operators and manufacturers were looking at the products of another supplier — American-owned Cummins, whose products had last been used by Dennis in the 1960s Maxim truck.

Cummins had long since abandoned its unpopular V-engines and was building a range of modern fuel-efficient in-line sixes. It was also looking to increase its European sales, partly with engines built at its two British plants in Shotts and Darlington.

Armed with details of the Cummins range, Dennis's designers sat down with a clean sheet of paper and decided to make a serious bid to produce a chassis which would satisfy growing demands from coach operators for a vehicle which was light but durable — and economical in operation.

The quest for economy was paramount. In the high inflation of the early 1980s British coach operators had been subsidising their operating costs with the profits made by selling their second-hand coaches at higher prices than they had paid for them. When the inflationary bubble burst, Dennis set out to produce a model in which the savings in fuel costs would cover the incremental costs which operators were facing in higher interest rates on money borrowed to fund the purchase of new coaches.

Rear-engined coaches had had a mixed reception in Britain. They had one advantage over conventional mid-engined designs and that was their luggage capacity, with massive storage space within the wheelbase beneath the floor. Most British operators preferred the handling and stability of mid-engined chassis, but the engine and gearbox took up much of the space between the front and rear axles, limiting luggage capacity.

Dennis's solution to this problem looked so simple that it seemed surprising it hadn't been tried before: move the engine as far back in the wheelbase as possible. The result was the all-new Javelin, which had a 240bhp turbocharged Cummins C-series 8.3-litre engine mounted vertically in the wheelbase but set right back, leaving plenty of luggage space ahead of the engine and retaining a rear boot as well. The frame was canted up in the wheelbase to maximise the space under the floor.

Up till now, Dennis had generally been a small player in British coaching. Yes, it had sold Dorchesters and Lancets and even a few Falcons, but in the grand scheme of things the numbers were low. With the Javelin, all this changed. It challenged the importers who were winning an increasing share of Britain's coach market and it quickly won a following amongst small companies. By 1994 Dennis had sold 1,300 — and to a wider variety of buyers than ever before. Major orders came from Stagecoach and the Minstry of Defence, but the Javelin's real strength was with a large number of small coach companies who found it a remarkably fuel-efficient coach, frequently recording figures in the region of 14mpg. Small numbers of Javelins were sold as buses.

The Javelin was but the start of an association with Cummins which was to spawn a range of new models in the late 1980s and early 1990s, taking Dennis to the position where it would be building more bus chassis than at any time in its 100-year history. Cummins engines featured in new models, and its L10 was offered as an option to Gardner power in the Dominator and, at 280bhp, in the export Dragon.

As the 1980s drew to a close, the Dennis bus chassis range was narrowed down. The success of the new Javelin quickly rendered both the Dorchester and the Lancet redundant.

Orders for double-deckers in the UK were dwindling in the late 1980s as the bus industry coped with the rigours of deregulation and privatisation, but the Dominator continued to find buyers, and in Hong Kong the Dragon was still selling well — by now adapted to handle a new generation of air-conditioned bodies. Small numbers of Falcon buses were being sold too, but operators were — temporarily at least — moving away from big single-deckers.

Now the team running Dennis really were going places, under managing director Steve Burton. The company had a clear product development programme, geared directly to the changing markets it was working in — and it was paying dividends.

However for the multi-faceted Hestair group, vehicle-building was no longer an area of major interest. In the early 1980s vehicle-related activities accounted for 75 per cent of the group's business. By 1988 its vehicle activities were still the same size, but were only 25 per cent of the business. Hestair had a growing interest in employment agencies — a growth area in the mid-1980s.

It had during its ownership of Dennis invested steadily in new models. However, this investment was a major drain on the company's funds — to develop and launch the Javelin, for example, took virtually all available working capital. And with the stock market collapse in the autumn of 1987 companies of all sizes — including Hestair — were finding it difficult to raise funds externally. The finance for future new models had to be generated internally.

In 1988 talks were held with AWD of Dunstable (the new owners of the former Bedford truck plant) but these negotiations did not produce new owners for Dennis and the other Hestair vehicle operations. However, yet again, a new direction for Dennis was around the corner.

Overleaf:
The Javelin chassis heralded Dennis's successful return to high-volume coach chassis production.

Javelin

PREMIUM COACH CHASSIS

Market Leadership

From cottage industry to world player

In 1988 Hestair not only owned Dennis in Guildford. It also owned Dennis Eagle in Warwick, Duple in Blackpool and Duple Metsec in Oldbury. At the 1988 Motor Show it reached agreement whereby its entire transport interests were to be bought out by Trinity Holdings, a new company set up by the directors of Hestair's vehicle interests under the leadership of Geoff Hollyhead (Dennis Eagle), along with Steve Burton (Dennis), Richard Owen (Duple) and Brendan Geary (Dennis Eagle's finance director).

Below:
Dominator sales continued in the 1990s, although the main thrust of production was switched to single-deckers. A Greater Manchester Buses Dominator passes a Domino midibus.

Left:
The Dart midi has been Britain's best-selling bus in the 1990s. Lothian Region Transport, the main operator in Edinburgh, runs 12.

Below:
London was the scene of the Dart's original success, revolutionising services in many parts of the capital. There are now over 800 Darts in London service.

The new management believed that given the freedom to develop products to match market needs, a healthy future lay ahead for the engineering group. This judgement was backed by Citicorp and Bankers Trust and the new ownership was established for £27 million, leaving Hestair free to pursue its own service businesses.

Trinity Holdings took the operations over in January 1989 and developed further the philosophy of producing world-class products designed to offer their users clear advantages over those from other vehicle builders. Under Hestair the company had moved away from being a manufacturer to being an assembler of high quality bought-in components which, of course, was the original philosophy of the

High passenger appeal, passenger comfort and swift performance attract custom and maximise revenues. Highly competitive pricing means operators can afford to increase service frequency for a given investment — attracting yet more business.
— *Dart brochure*

Dennis brothers almost 100 years earlier.

Almost immediately the new management were hit hard by a shrinking market and low-priced competition, and the Duple coachbuilding factory in Blackpool was closed. But the remaining operations have flourished under Trinity ownership, with group output and profitability showing significant year-on-year growth. Since 1985 Dennis Eagle has been building the Dennis range of refuse collection vehicles, where originally Eagle was simply a body manufacturer. The Dennis Eagle range was expanded in 1992 with the launch of the Elite, an all-new purpose-designed refuse vehicle which quickly became a best-seller. The Elite has a modern low-built stainless-steel cab, set ahead of the front axle, to provide easy access for the crew.

Duple Metsec has continued exporting body kits, often for fitment to Dennis chassis with considerable success, including a large order for 2,500 buses for Sri Lanka.

For Dennis Specialist Vehicles, as the Guildford operation now traded, the change in ownership was quickly followed by relocation of the factory. Buses and fire engines were still being built on part of the original Dennis Brothers site at Woodbridge Hill, which although it had been modernised over the years wasn't ideally suited to efficient manufacture. And although Britain was in the grip of the worst economic recession for decades, Dennis was sufficiently confident in its products to be planning a programme of expansion.

A green field site was identified in the north-east of the town and a new purpose-built factory with a planned capacity of three times the then current sales volumes was opened in 1990, starting off with a workforce of 317. As well as building Javelins, Dominators, Falcons and fire appliances, it was to be fully occupied

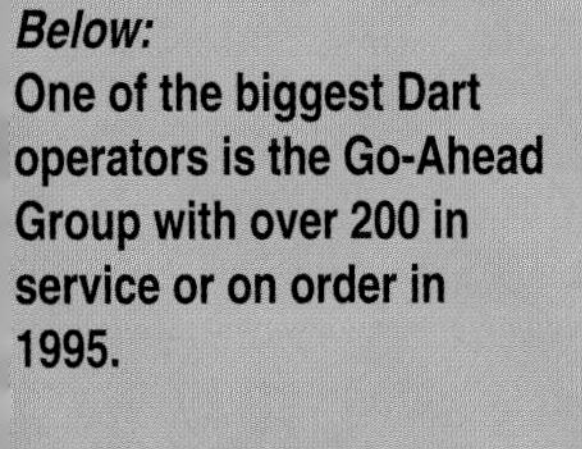

Below:
One of the biggest Dart operators is the Go-Ahead Group with over 200 in service or on order in 1995.

Left:
The Dart was designed for export markets too. Berkhof bodied this one for service in Holland.

Below:
Production of refuse collection vehicles became the responsibility of sister company Dennis Eagle. Its Elite model won new customers in Britain and spearheaded export sales of special-purpose municipal and airside vehicles.

with the development of a new model which was one of the most successful in Dennis's history.

Deregulation of British bus operation had come in 1986 and turned 50 years of comparative stability on its head. In the new competitive environment many operators had invested in minibuses in a bid to retain existing passengers and win new ones. Van-derived minibuses was not a market in which Dennis was interested — but research showed that many operators wanted something bigger. Not a full-sized bus, but a midibus which would preserve something of the friendly atmosphere of the minibus but would at the same time be more durable, offer a better quality ride and carry more passengers.

The model which Dennis developed to meet this new market was a runaway success. It was the Dart, initially conceived as a 9m 39-seater, and then developed as a shorter 8.5m 35-seater and a bigger 9.8m 43-seater. The first prototypes were completed in 1988 and the first Dart to enter service did so in 1989 — significantly the operator was London Buses.

London had not been deregulated, but there were changes in the way routes were managed, with competitive tendering opening up opportunities for new operators. And London Buses had an ageing fleet of 1960s Routemaster double-deckers to replace. They might have represented the typical London bus, but with the need for a two-person crew were expensive to operate.

Factors such as these were making London Buses managers look at new ways of operating. High-frequency services with high-quality small buses was one of the options they decided to pursue. And the Dart was the bus they used — in big numbers.

The Dart used Cummins's 5.9-litre B-series engine and was bodied by all of Britain's leading coachbuilders, each of which designed bodywork specifically for the new Dennis model.

It quickly became a best-seller, not only in terms of Dennis's output, but in terms of the

UK bus market as a whole where in the early 1990s it notched up more sales than any model from any other bus manufacturer. Just as the Javelin had brought new customers to Dennis, so to did the Dart. It very quickly established the company as the major supplier of buses to London, far outstripping any others. By the end of 1994 there were over 800 in service in the capital. It introduced Dennis to Lothian Region Transport, serving Edinburgh, Scotland's capital city. And it won the company large orders from four of the major bus groups in post-deregulation Britain — Badgerline, British Bus, the Go-Ahead Group and Stagecoach.

> Available in 10.6m and 11.6m variants, and designed to accommodate centre exits readily, the Dennis Lance is a further example of the Dennis design philosophy which has created a full range of best-selling bus and coach products. Sophisticated componentry in a deceptively simple layout adds up to a highly efficient street machine which is easy to drive, easy to maintain, and profitable to operate.
> — *Lance brochure, 1992*

The Dart was also the choice for some unusual operations. Feeder services to London's fast-growing City Airport were introduced by Darts. And when the Channel Tunnel opened for business in the summer of 1994, the vehicles which were chosen to provide transport at Folkestone for truck drivers using the Le Shuttle Freight service were also Darts.

Many operators looked to the Dart to replace conventional single-deckers, such as Ulsterbus in Northern Ireland, Go-Ahead Northern in the north-east of England, and Isle of Man Transport. And while orders from big fleets were rolling in, so too were orders from small businesses throughout the British Isles — and beyond.

Below:
An air-conditioned Dart pioneered a successful Hong Kong sales drive.

Above:
The Lance is available with bodywork by all of Britain's leading bodybuilders. This Ipswich bus has Optare bodywork.

The first export Darts went to Kowloon Motor Bus in Hong Kong, by now an established Dennis user. These were followed by the first left-hand-drive version, bodied in Holland by Berkhof and sold to NZH after a period of evaluation. Then in 1994 in a unique agreement with Swedish manufacturer Scania, the first Darts were sold in Australia to Invicta in Melbourne. For the Australian market Scania Australia imports Dart kits from Guildford which are assembled in Scania Australia's modern plant in Melbourne.

In the export double-deck business, the attractions of the three-axle high-capacity Dragon were not lost on another company which became an important Dennis user in the 1990s: the Stagecoach group. The first new double-deck buses ever to operate in Malawi came from Dennis — ten Dragons for Stagecoach Malawi which needed big buses for a trunk service in the capital city, Blantyre. These were soon followed by similar buses for operation by Stagecoach in Kenya's capital, Nairobi.

Having gained so much new ground with both Javelin and Dart, Dennis decided to develop another new model — again with an eye to anticipated market trends. This was a single-decker which would use the Dart philosophy of simple engineering but in a bigger vehicle. The new model was to be both lighter and less expensive than the Falcon, which it would ultimately replace.

The new Lance, launched in 1991, used the same engine as the Javelin, but rated at a more modest 211bhp and now mounted vertically in the rear overhang. The engine was sufficiently compact to sit under the rear row of seats. The first two customers to place orders — Kowloon Motor Bus and London Buses — gave some indication of the Lance's broad appeal. Within three years of its launch it had become the standard single-decker in the Badgerline group, had won repeat orders from London Buses — and had formed the basis of yet another revolutionary new model.

The Lance, like most rear-engined single-deck chassis, offered a fairly low floor height and an entrance with low steps. However any steps at all can impede access for people with

Above:
Some of the first Lance orders came from London Buses.

disabilities and certainly put public transport out of bounds for wheelchair users — as well as making life difficult for mothers with push-chairs. To address this a new breed of ultra-low-floor buses was making its appearance in Europe. Complex drivelines were being used to obtain a flat floor — and were pushing up both production costs and selling prices to a level which was unacceptable to British operators who did not enjoy the same level of public subsidy as their mainland European counterparts.

The idea of totally accessible buses appealed to many leading British fleets — but the economics of their operation was a strong disincentive to experiment with them. Dennis had the answer. By fitting independent front suspension in a chassis frame which retained the conventional Lance rear end, the company was able to offer a chassis on which the front two-thirds of the floor — the area ahead of the rear axle — would be step-free.

The use of the Lance driveline kept costs down. The use of independent front suspension kept the floor level down. The

Evolution through the Javelin's modular design has taken it from a 211bhp medium-weight bus or lightweight coach replacement through to a 240bhp all-purpose vehicle.

Not only was the GX the first full-size coach to beat the 12mpg barrier on *Coach and Bus Week* road test but it did it with ease.

Drivers jumping from the 240bhp-engined Javelin to the GX will notice the extra surge from that extra 50bhp. As the needle enters the green it is like turning a tap on and it pulls right through to maximum revs.

— from a road test of a 290bhp Javelin GX in Coach and Bus Week, *1994*

Lance SLF, indicating Super Low Floor, could accommodate pushchairs, shopping trolleys and travellers in wheelchairs. Immediately London Buses placed an order, which saw Britain's first totally-accessible bus service get under way in the capital's western suburbs at the start of 1994, with further services following during the year.

Further orders for the SLF came from the Go-Ahead Group in north-east England, from Stagecoach and from the British Airports Authority at London's Heathrow Airport. The Stagecoach vehicles were used to upgrade a park-and-ride service in historic Canterbury — and to demonstrate to motorists just how good modern buses could be.

Meanwhile there were developments on the coach front with a new model launch in 1993 to broaden the appeal of the Javelin range which now included 8.5, 10 and 11m models. This was the flagship Javelin GX, Dennis's most powerful coach ever. It was introduced to meet operator demands for a higher specification chassis and it not only offered more power — 290bhp — but came with front disc brakes and uprated suspension to allow for the heavier high-floor bodies which tour operators were demanding for operations to mainland Europe. The disc brake installation drew on the company's experience in building fire appliances.

The new model development

Dramatically improving the standards of roadholding, manoeuvrability, acceleration and braking, the Dennis Rapier is the drivers' machine.

Superb performance derives from an entirely new order of advanced chassis design.

The Dennis Rapier has a rigid 'space-frame' construction manufactured from Cromweld. It's lighter, stiffer and lower than a conventional 'ladder-frame' — so that's less weight to haul around, the roll rate is reduced, and handling is much more positive.
— *Rapier brochure, 1993*

Left:
The Lance SLF is the most sophisticated bus yet built in Britain, offering easy passenger access while retaining a simple and reliable driveline. Over 100 were in service in 1995.

Below:
New standards of performance and handling have been set by the award-winning Rapier.

was not confined to bus and coach chassis. In 1991 the Rapier was launched and represented a complete break with previous generations of fire appliances — although these remained in production. Gone was the conventional chassis frame and in its place a welded tubular spaceframe produced using Cromweld. This gave a low frame height and eased the fitment of independent front suspension with disc brakes. Power came from a 250bhp Cummins C-series 8.3-litre engine driving through an Allison five-speed automatic gearbox.

The rear axle had coil spring suspension and the wheels were 19.5in instead of 22in. Standard features included anti-lock brakes and traction control. The result was an appliance with a low centre of gravity and umatched performance, not just in straight-line acceleration to its 75mph top speed, but in the all-important areas of cornering and braking. New technology is never cheap, but a test drive in the Rapier was enough to convince a good number of fire chiefs that here was a vehicle safer than any other they had ever tried.

The Rapier soon found buyers amongst brigades in Britain — and re-established Dennis as a supplier of fire-appliances in the hotly contested mainland European market. In 1994 it won a prestigious British Design Award.

There were changes at Trinity too. After four years of successful growth at all of its subsidiaries — but particularly at Dennis, Trinity Holdings was launched as a public company on the London stock market in October 1992. Despite the poor economic outlook because of problems with Britain's relationship with the European exchange rate

TWO MODERN
SUITES
0272
252276
300
BRISTOL
BADGERLINE
129
BADGERLINE
DENNIS
PLAXTON
L129 TFB

Left:
One of Britain's biggest bus groups, Badgerline, standardised on Darts and Lances for its single-deck fleet. This is a Lance with Plaxton Verde bodywork.

Below:
The 290bhp Javelin GX has won Dennis many new customers.

mechanism, the shares were almost three times over-subscribed. Expansion by Trinity at the start of the 1990s saw the acquisition of specialist fire appliance bodybuilders Carmichael, and of Reliance Mercury, the towing tractor makers which had been bought by Dennis in 1964 and sold by Hestair 10 years later.

A significant expansion of overseas activity was announced in 1993, coming on stream in mid-1994. This was Dennis's first joint venture company, UMW Dennis in Malaysia, where a new factory was built to assemble Dennis Dart, Lance and Javelin bus chassis (along with Duple Metsec bodies) for the Malaysian market. Initial output was 20 vehicles a month. Dennis identified the Pacific Rim as an area offering considerable growth potential, and a joint venture with local production as a more attractive option than the expensive shipping of completed vehicles.

As the company approached its centenary year, one more new product was coming on stream — the Sabre. This is a replacement for the long-lived RS/SS range of fire appliances which utilises the stylish Rapier cab structure but on a conventional ladder-frame chassis. The Sabre has front disc brakes, a 250bhp Cummins engine and an Allison five-speed automatic gearbox with power take-off. The first was sold to the Joint Fire Services (Wiltshire) consortium.

Thus 1995 sees Dennis with a broad range of modern bus and coach chassis — Dart, Lance, Lance SLF, Javelin, Javelin GX, Dominator and Dragon — selling to a growing number of customers of all sizes both in Britain and abroad. These are produced in a modern purpose-built factory, alongside the Rapier and the Sabre.

Many famous truck and bus builders have vanished over the years through the relentless

processes of take-overs, mergers and closures. And there have always been industry analysts quick to say that small manufacturers cannot survive. But in its centenary year Dennis has proved otherwise, by having the right products at the right time. Its growth has been a major factor in the success of Trinity Holdings which is debt free and has a market value of around £160 million — six times its 1989 level.

Dennis enters its 100th year as UK market leader in city buses, enjoying increasing share in a growing market. In 1994 it sold its 2,000th Dart and 1,000th Javelin — and continued to increase both UK and export sales. Over 1,100 bus chassis were built in 1994, breaking the previous bus and truck production record set in 1949. The company is also UK market leader in fire appliances, with the technically-advanced Rapier demonstrating to a growing number of brigades the superiority of a purpose-designed appliance over those built on modified truck chassis.

All in all, it's the sort of achievement John and Raymond Dennis would have saluted.

Above:
Dennis has built up a substantial business exporting giant three-axle double-deckers to operators in the Far East and Africa. This Dragon is in service in Hong Kong.

> One of the biggest surprises of the Dart is its turning circle — it needs very little space in front of it to make a clean getaway without reversing. Turning into tight corners really poses no problems and it would be at home on a minibus route provided the gaps are enough for its 2.35m width.
> *— from a road test in* Buses, *December 1990*

Top:
The Lance helped open up new export markets in the Far East and in Europe: a Lance and Dart operating for NZH in Holland. *M. Fowler*

Above:
Stagecoach, Britain's biggest bus operator, bought both Javelins and, as shown here, Darts.

Major Dennis bus and coach users in the 1990s

Badgerline group
- Badgerline
- Brewers
- Bristol City Line
- Eastern National
- Midland Red West
- South Wales Transport
- Thamesway
- United Welsh
- Western National

Bournemouth Transport
Brighton Transport
British Airports Authority
British Bus group
- Clydeside 2000
- London & Country
- Midland Red North
- North Western

Busways Travel Services
Caldaire Holdings
- West Riding
- Yorkshire Buses

Capital Citybus, London
Capital Coaches, London
Chester City Transport
China Motor Bus
County Bus & Coach
D Coaches, Swansea
Derby City Transport
Eastbourne Buses
Eastern Counties
Epsom Coaches
Go-Ahead group
- Coastline
- Go-Ahead Gateshead
- Gypsy Queen
- Northern
- VFM Buses
- Wear Buses

Go-Whittle, Kidderminster
Great Yarmouth Transport
Greater Manchester Buses
Grey-Green, London
Grimsby-Cleethorpes Transport
Invicta, Melbourne
Ipswich Buses
Jones Motors, Pontypridd
Kelvin Central Buses
Kentish Bus
G K Kinch, Loughborough
Kingston upon Hull Transport
Kowloon Motor Bus
Leicester Citybus
Lincolnshire Road Car
London Buses
- CentreWest
- East London
- London Central
- London General
- London Northern
- London United
- Metroline
- Selkent
- South London
- Westlink

London Country North West
Lothian Region Transport
McGill's Bus Service, Barrhead
Mainline, Sheffield
A Mayne & Sons, Manchester
Metrobus, Orpington
Moor-Dale, Newcastle
NZH, Holland
North Devon
Plymouth Citybus
PMT
Q Drive Buses, Bracknell
R&I Buses, London
Redwing Coaches, London
Rhondda Buses
Safeguard, Guildford
Southampton Citybus
Southern National
Stagecoach group
- Bluebird Buses
- Coastline Buses
- East Kent
- Fife Scottish
- Hampshire Bus
- Inverness Traction
- Kenya Bus Services
- Ribble
- South Coast Buses
- Stagecoach Malawi
- United Counties

Strathtay Scottish
Tayside Public Transport
Thames Transit
Thamesdown Transport
Transit Holdings
Ulsterbus
Warrington Transport
West Midlands Travel
Western Scottish
Yorkshire Rider
Yorkshire Terrier
Yorkshire Traction

Appendix 2
Dennis model names

Ace	small bus chassis, introduced 1933
Ajax	2-3 ton lorry, introduced 1937
Alleycat	narrow refuse collection lorry, 1970s
Arrow	high-powered bus and coach chassis, introduced 1930; low-volume mid-engined chassis for South Africa, late 1970s
Bulkmaster	1970s refuse collection vehicle
Centaur	lorry, 1950-56
Condor	lorry, 1956-62; 1980s three-axle rear-engined double-deck bus chassis
Dart	small bus chassis introduced 1929; front-engined bus, late 1970s; new-generation midibus chassis, introduced 1989
Defiant	front-engined export bus, mid-1960s; 24 ton tractive unit, 1970-72
Delta	1963 fire appliance; 1970s 16 ton export truck and bus chassis
Dominant	mid-engined bus chassis, 1951-52; rigid truck, 1970-72
Dominator	rear-engined double-deck bus chassis, launched 1978
Domino	heavy-duty rear-engined midibus, 1984-85
Dragon	1948 tractive unit; 1980s three-axle rear-engined double-deck bus chassis
Falcon	light bus chassis, 1939-57; rear-engined citybus chassis, 1980-93
Firebird	Delta-based export fire appliance
Gladiator	planned early 1950s heavy-duty export bus chassis; none were built
Hefty	14 ton lorry, 1956-60
Heron	light commercial, 1955-64
Horla	Pax derivative for articulated operation, 1946-59
Javelin	new generation coach chassis, launched 1986
Jubilant	12 ton lorry 1946-61; 1970s export double-deck bus chassis
Lance	double-deck bus chassis, 1930-54; rear-engined urban bus chassis introduced 1990
Lancet	single-deck bus chassis, 1931-60; midrange bus/coach chassis 1980-1988
Loline	lowheight bus chassis, 1956-67
Mace	development of Ace, built 1934-37
Max	7-8 ton lorry, 1937-56
Max Major	twin-steer lorry, 1939
Max Six	six-cylinder Max model, 1949-56
Maxim	30 ton tractive unit, introduced 1964
Onslow	used briefly for F1 fire appliance chassis
Pacamatic	1960s refuse collection vehicle
Pactum	1930s refuse collection vehicle
Paragon	lawn mower
Paravan	urban delivery vehicle, introduced 1958
Pax	postwar 5-ton-plus model
Paxit	1950s refuse collection vehicle
Paxit Major	1950s refuse collection vehicle
Pelican	lightweight mid-engined bus chassis, 1956
Phoenix	refuse collection vehicle
Pike	bus variant of Ajax lorry
Rapier	high-specification fire appliance, launched 1991
Sabre	fire appliance, launched 1995
Stork	lightweight mid-engined chassis, 1953-59
Swallow	lawn mower
Teal	export bus chassis, 1950s
Tippax	1950s refuse collection vehicle
Triton	bus based on Pax goods chassis
Vendor	prototype front-wheel-drive light van, 1960
Vulture	mid-1950s refuse collector
Waterbird	Delta-based export water tanker